Vicarage

The Rocks

Sackville College
Almshouse
(Endowed A.D. 1616.)

St. Swithin's Church
(Vicarage)

CHURCH STREET

B.M. 451·8   Grave Yard

B.M. 434·1

Letter Box

Dorset Arms Hotel

P

P

P

Detail from 25-inch
Ordnance Survey map, 1873.

799

100 BUILDINGS
of East Grinstead

100 BUILDINGS
of East Grinstead

M.J. LEPPARD

PHILLIMORE

2006

Published by
PHILLIMORE & CO. LTD
Shopwyke Manor Barn, Chichester, West Sussex, England
www.phillimore.co.uk

ISBN 1-86077-381-8
ISBN 13 978-1-86077-381-5

Printed and bound in Great Britain by
CAMBRIDGE PRINTING

Frontispiece: View from the parish church tower in the 1950s, looking south-west over the High Street and showing several of the buildings featured in this book. (East Grinstead Observer)

CONTENTS

ACKNOWLEDGEMENTS

The author is grateful to the following for permission to reproduce photographs: East Grinstead Town Museum: 3, 8 (both illustrations), 11 (portrait), 12, 13, 14, 15, 17, 18, 19, 21, 24, 27, 28, 30, 31, 33, 38, 40 (portrait), 44, 45, 51 (both illustrations), 52, 54, 55 (both illustrations), 56 (portrait) 60, 61, 66 (three illustrations), 67, 72, 74 (exterior and Sister Ermenild), 77, 78, 82 (portrait), 87, 90, 92, 93 (portrait), 95, 96, 97, 98; Mr M. Powell (who took over Harold Connold's business and still has his negatives): 9, 13, 16, 17, 56 (portrait), 92; Miss R.M. Willatts: 15, 30, 97; The East Grinstead Society, 16 (family portrait), 19, 21, 33, 38, 46; *The East Grinstead Courier*: 36, 76, 94, 99; Mr M.J. Berry 42; Mr N. Sherry 45; *The East Grinstead Observer*, 11 (portrait), 51 (portrait), 54, 79; Mr M. Green 71; Mr D. Pocock 10; Mr D. Mould 93. All other illustrations are from the author's own collection. If I have unwittingly infringed any rights, I apologise.

I am grateful to the editor of the *East Grinstead Courier* for the suggestion that led to the series of articles that form the basis of this book and encouraging their republication in revised and more permanent form, to her colleagues for their collaboration at every stage and for lending the photographs credited to the paper above. I am equally grateful to those readers who sent in corrections or supplementary information, especially Mrs Beth Chase Grey for the bulk of the article on Woodcock. Thanks are also due to Mr M.J. Berry, Mr D. Pocock and the Town Museum for lending the illustrations credited to them and to Mr S.R. Kerr for taking for me contemporary photographs of buildings for which none of any age could be found. The credit for presenting everything so impressively belongs entirely to my publishers, Phillimore, for which I thank them, as also for their courtesy and encouragement at every stage.

INTRODUCTION

This book originated as a series of one hundred articles, 'Buildings with a History', published weekly in the *East Grinstead Courier* from 27 March 2003 to 17 February 2005.

The buildings selected are not the hundred best (however defined) or oldest, nor the most important, most aesthetically pleasing or most architecturally or historically significant, nor are they all listed, or even necessarily the author's favourites. Each, however, has something of interest to be told about it, whether in any of those categories or because of people or events with which it has been associated.

As with my *A History of East Grinstead* (Phillimore, 2001), which provides an historical context for the buildings discussed here, I have drawn on over four decades of research, so that much previously unpublished information will be found in these pages. I have taken the opportunity to revise the original newspaper articles, correcting where necessary and incorporating some information discovered after writing them. For each building I have indicated, where it exists, other published work giving more detail, usually including source references. These notes, at the end of the book, give some assurance of academic respectability without, I hope, detracting from readability by acknowledging every source used. As far as possible the illustrations are ones that have not already appeared in published works. The index of place-names serves simultaneously for illustrations and buildings, including those mentioned incidentally in the text of featured buildings. There is also an index of personal names.

To protect the privacy and security of owners of and residents in private houses, I have not included any buildings that cannot be seen from public roads or footpaths, nor mentioned any of their contents.

This book therefore affords no pretext for any intrusion into their grounds.

The random order of the original articles has been replaced by topographical sequences in which each building is located in relation to the one preceding it. Detailed familiarity with East Grinstead is thus not taken for granted, and locating the buildings on a map or taking short walks or bus or car trips to see them for oneself is facilitated. The first six sequences start from, and in some cases return to, the parish church, as the most easily identifiable and accessible point of reference. The seventh is within Forest Row, the eighth in Ashurst Wood, while the last is a clockwise list of the more outlying buildings, for which national grid references are given in the text as further aid to location. I have followed paths rather than roads where possible and indicated in general terms where public transport access is available. All the buildings are within the area covered by the Ordnance Survey's 1:25,000 (2½ inch) Explorer map 18, Ashdown Forest. An up-to-date street-map will be found in the official town guide, revised every two years.

This book is by no means a trail, however; it is too selective and too detailed for that. Moreover the built-up area is already comprehensively covered by the town trails published by the East Grinstead Society: no.1 the High Street conservation area, no.2 19th- and 20th-century town centre, no.3 Victorian heritage around the centre. Their necessarily brief notes will supplement these pages, as will Dorothy Hatswell's *Walk around Historic East Grinstead* (Frith Book Company, 2005), a well-illustrated and companionable volume, though not without a few factual lapses.

SEQUENCES

1 The parish church north-eastwards to **11** *The Guinea Pig* (from which buses to the town centre on weekdays).

12 Nos 51-3 High Street eastwards to **17** Woodbury and back westwards from **18** Barton St Mary to **28** Middle Row.

29 Wilmington House westwards to **45** railway viaduct. (Buses to the town centre from the nearby stop in Brooklands Way on weekdays.)

46 No.39 High Street north-westwards to **62** Felbridge bridge and back south-eastwards to **70** the Post Office building. (Buses to the town centre from the stop near the bridge outside the hotel.)

71 The new town museum northwards to **74** the Old Convent.

75 Dovecotes and the Gatehouse southwards to **79** Saint Hill. (Buses serve the Standen drive and Saint Hill Green.)

80 Forest Row Village Hall circular to **85** Brambletye Castle. (Buses between East Grinstead and the village centre via Ashurst Wood.)

86 St Dunstan's, **87** Ashurst Wood Abbey and **88** *The Three Crowns.*

89 Little Shovelstrode Hall clockwise to **100** Woodcock. (Buses between East Grinstead and Crawley serve Felbridge School; very infrequent weekday buses pass Woodcock; no buses near other places in this sequence except as indicated for Kingscote station.)

Where there is incidental mention of a building that has an entry of its own, the number of that entry is given in square brackets to permit easy cross-reference.

I shall be glad to receive observations, corrections and further information from readers and will do my best to answer questions. Those who wish to talk about the book are advised that my name is pronounced the same way as that of the animal.

If this book enhances understanding and appreciation of East Grinstead and its surroundings, if local people see familiar structures in a new light, if strangers think there is something here worth visiting, and if posterity judges that valuable information that might otherwise have been lost has been recorded, I shall consider my efforts worthwhile.

M.J. Leppard, January 2006

THE BUILDINGS

The northern side of the parish church in 1911.
On the left is the vicarage, designed by the diocesan
architect Lacy W. Ridge to replace the one burnt down
in 1908 and itself replaced in 1965.

PARISH CHURCH OF ST SWITHUN

There has been a church on this hill-top site where several ancient tracks met for something over a thousand years. Until 1836 it was the church for Ashurst Wood and Forest Row as well as the town and surrounding countryside, a parish of over 15,000 acres, nearly 25 square miles.

The present building was put up over the period 1789-1813 following the collapse of the tower on the body of the church in 1785. The leading architect James Wyatt, who had already worked not far away at Sheffield Place, was engaged but fund-raising was slow, requiring an Act of Parliament in 1790 authorising trustees to borrow the necessary sum. Before the tower could be built the money ran out, so another Act was needed, in 1811, and a new architect appointed to design it, William Inwood.

The church Wyatt designed was on the usual 18th-century plan but in the fashionable 'Gothick' style and with some respect for its medieval predecessor. In 1874 the present interior layout began to take shape, including an area for the choir, followed in the first half of the 20th century by side-chapels and an organ in the singing gallery.

Like all ancient parish churches it always had secular functions as well as religious, including housing a school in the 16th and 18th centuries and the parish fire engine in the early nineteenth. Today the tradition continues, mainly with concerts, and the church normally hosts the special services for big occasions that usually bring all denominations together. At the same time it maintains the regular round of daily and Sunday worship and is always open during the working day for those who want a quiet space in the centre of the town.

The church is an imposing building, with an impressive tower that can be seen from many miles away, listed as of architectural or historical importance, grade 2, and currently working through another of the inevitable periodic restoration programmes. It is the only one in Sussex with 13 bells and contains several interesting monuments, stained glass windows and other furnishings, including a few items from its predecessor.

The monuments in the churchyard are also worth looking at, including that to John Mason Neale, warden of Sackville College [16] 1846-66, and the memorial slabs to the three people burnt to death in East Grinstead in 1556 as Protestant heretics.

St Swithun, to whom the church is dedicated, was bishop of Winchester from 852 to 862 and one of the most popular saints of the second half of the 10th century. His feast day is 15 July.

Inside the church, looking east, following the fall of the tower, after an original painted 16-17 November 1785 by James Lambert.

THE CHURCHYARD WALL IN CHURCH LANE

The eastern wall of the churchyard, purely functional and seldom glanced at by passers-by, is of interest for the way it was built and the historical reasons for its present appearance.

It clearly consists of self-contained sections, varying in style and materials not only from their neighbours but also within themselves. The reason is that, historically, different lengths of churchyard walls or fences were the responsibility of particular estates within each parish. The owners of those lands had to repair the wall at their own expense, with whatever materials they had available, could afford or liked the look of. Usually, as here, the result was a patchwork, random yet not unattractive because the use of local brick or stone ensured some overall coherence.

The last attempt to enforce those duties in East Grinstead was in 1869 when the vestry, the ratepayers' representative body, called on Mr Capes of Brockhurst to repair the gateway by the *Rose and Crown* [13]. Mr Capes, a Roman Catholic, refused to do so and the vestry made its own arrangements since the recently-closed churchyard was now legally its responsibility. In 1952 upkeep of the churchyard was taken over by the Urban District Council, a task inherited by the Town Council in 1974.

In his account of the wall Hills gives the properties, their owners and tenants and the lengths for which they were responsible as itemised in 1711. The list does not account for the full circuit.

Perhaps the wall is of sufficient age, interest and comparative rarity to deserve listing, as the arch over the south entrance to the churchyard already is.

One other noteworthy feature is the different levels of churchyard and road here. While traffic wears down roads, centuries of burials raise churchyard surfaces.

The wall in June 2005, showing different sections and varied materials, photographed for this book by S.R. Kerr.

COTTAGES IN CHURCH LANE

Property in Church Lane has been called the Old Almshouses since at least 1599, when William Kidder bequeathed it to his son Jeremy. Obviously by then it was privately owned and had lost its original charitable function of housing needy elderly or poor people. There can be no doubt that it is the almshouse for three persons founded early in the 16th century by Dame Katherine Grey and her second husband Richard Lewkenor of Brambletye, as recorded on their memorial brass in the parish church. That side of Church Lane lay in the tithing of Brambletye, so the site was within their jurisdiction as well as conveniently located for the almsfolk's material requirements to be met in the town and their spiritual needs in the church.

The title deeds reveal that these cottages replace older ones that had burnt down in 1720 or earlier. They remained in residential use until taken over for extra office space by the solicitors in the more substantial house to the north, no.8, in 1967.

On Thursday 23 March in that year, the day after the last carpet had been laid in the new offices, a fire caused serious damage to the roof of no.8 but no important documents were destroyed and it was business as usual next morning. The origin of that building, which was leased as the second home of the newly-founded Sisterhood of St Margaret from 1856 to 58, is recorded on a stone in the back wall: 'Richard and Jane Austen, 1763'. It has been used as solicitors' offices since 1876.

The whole complex is listed grade 2 and within the conservation area.

The cottages in Church Lane and their neighbours, c.1905, with Mrs Ada Mason (born 1881) and her son George (born 1900).

THE PARISH HALLS, De La Warr Road

For years the Parish Halls, at the far end of Church Lane, were our principal public halls and, after the bombing of the *Whitehall* [49] in 1943, for long the only place suitable for theatrical productions. The Operatic Society performed Gilbert and Sullivan on the tiny stage, with the chorus swaying rhythmically for want of space to dance. For most of the Second World War the building was occupied by Canadian troops, who left some saucy murals on the kitchen wall.

The Large Hall was erected in 1929 at a cost of over £4,000 after extensive fund-raising by members of the parish church. Its architect, John D. Clarke, intended it 'should have a homely atmosphere [and] be light and cheery, and to some extent exhilarating'.

It occupied the site of the worn-out main part of the similarly financed Parish Room opened on 28 December 1899 on part of the former Chequer Mead, a field once associated with the *Chequer* inn in the High Street. The rooms originally known as the soup kitchen and classroom remained until replaced by the present Small Hall, completed in 1933 for almost £2,000. With a club room above and a committee room and kitchen between it and the main hall, additional and more varied space for church activities was provided, subsidised by lettings to other bodies.

The original trust deed made the vicar and churchwardens *ex officio* trustees and specified that the building was 'for the benefit of the parish of East Grinstead', wording said to have been carefully chosen to prevent their ever becoming diocesan property. However, by 1958 there were two factions among the trustees, one headed by the vicar, the Rev. H.C.F. Copsey, insisting this meant the ecclesiastical parish, the other, headed by Mr T. Barrett of Barredale Court, arguing it meant the civil parish. For over twelve years the struggle went on, until a legal ruling that it was the civil parish that was to benefit, even though the construction had all been financed by the church. Accordingly the Urban District Council, the authority administering the civil parish, took over responsibility and a new hall for church purposes was built in the churchyard in 1971.

Today we have a theatre and several newer halls but the Town Council, as trustees succeeding the Urban District Council, still keeps the Parish Halls in good order and has no problem letting them for a great range of activities.

The Parish Halls from the south-south-east in June 2005, photographed for this book by S.R. Kerr.

CHEQUER MEAD ARTS CENTRE AND THEATRE

The schools seen from the south across the Playfield before Church Lane and De La Warr Road were extended in 1908.

Public meetings in 1859 led to the opening, in January 1861, of a National (i.e. Church) School in what is now the main block of our Arts Centre, diagonally opposite the Parish Halls. The site, part of Slaughterhouse Mead and worth £200, was given by Lady Amherst, Mr Parsons of Lewes was the architect, and the work was carried out in local sandstone by the East Grinstead builder Robert Pink. Boys were taught at the western end, girls at the eastern, with the headmaster's house in the centre. In 1865 a separate infants' school was erected on the west, now with a sheltered connection to the main building.

It ceased to be a denominational school in 1876, though the church remained the ground landlord. In 1882, once elementary schooling had become compulsory, a house for the master was built beside the infants' block and a building for the girls' classes behind it. On reorganisation in 1927 that block became the junior school and the boys' classrooms the senior, with mixed classes throughout. In 1951 the latter, by now a secondary modern, was given the name Sackville, after the most prominent family in East Grinstead's history, and the former was called Chequer Mead Primary School after a

nearby field rather than the one on which it stood. In 1964 Sackville moved from the increasingly inadequate premises to new ones in Lewes Road and Chequer Mead took over the vacated rooms. Two years later the rear block became the Wallis Centre for youth work, named after Miss Iris Wallis, for many years a leading figure in the girl guides and other provision for young people in the town.

When the primary school, renamed the Meads, moved to a new building in the Dunnings area in 1990 the buildings were transformed, on the initiative of the Town Council, into the splendid facility we enjoy today, including theatre, art gallery, café and meeting rooms. It was designed by the London architects Tim Ronalds, built by the local contractors Martin Smith & Foster, and officially opened on 17 November 1996. The total cost, including site acquisition and fees, was £2.41 million, of which the Town Council contributed £1.23 million, the District Council £500,000 and the national lottery £680,000. There was inevitably controversy about such use of public funds and the design of the extension accommodating the theatre but in 2000 it gained an award from the Royal Institute of British Architects.

THE PLAYFIELD WATER TOWER

One of East Grinstead's best known landmarks, sometimes mistaken from a distance for a church, is the water tower in a corner of the car park opposite the arts centre.

The car park was created in 1992 on the historic Playfield, known by that name since at least 1803 and long used undisputed for recreation and as a drying ground for domestic washing. In 1908 the Urban District Council acquired it from Earl De La Warr's trustees for £50 with its traditional uses unimpeded.

The fire brigade's inability to prevent the nearby vicarage burning down, owing to insufficient pressure in the water supply, on 27 February that year led the East Grinstead Gas and Water Company to plan a water tower on the nearest public open space, the Playfield, lest a similar fate befell timber-framed buildings in the High Street. The council ensured that it would be a dignified structure in keeping with neighbouring Sackville College [16]. The date of construction, 1914, is on the keystone over the door. Two stones at the north-west angle name the company's officers and directors, including W. Vaux Graham, their engineer, who presumably designed the tower, and the builders Messrs Norman & Burt of Burgess Hill.

The tower is 80 feet high and measures 24 square feet to the outside of the butresses. The tank at the top could hold 30,000 gallons of water.

During the Second World War the tower was used by the army or home guard as a look-out post with a machine-gun mounted on the turret and there was a static water tank in the opposite corner for fire-fighting.

By 1992, disused but listed grade 2 and in the conservation area, the tower was for sale by informal tender without guide price, 'offering potential for change of use'. Provided they signed a form accepting all responsibility, anyone interested could climb the iron staircase for the view from what the vendors gratuitously renamed the Sackville Water Tower.

The anonymous buyer was understood to be intending to convert it into a private residence but all that has happened so far is the removal of the tank in June 1998 and, despite protests and formal objections in 2002, the attachment of a mobile 'phone mast, antennae and ancillary equipment.

The water tower, seen from the north early in the 20th century.

ESTCOTS, off College Lane

A bridleway marked with a finger-post at the top entrance to East Court leads past the front garden of Estcots, a complete 15th-century hall house, rebuilt at its west end in the 16th century and extended to the north in the mid-seventeenth.

Its name, however, is far older, first recorded in 1285 and meaning cottage in the east. As an inhabited site it is probably much older still, sheltered from the prevailing winds and down a hollow lane just off the ancient, probably prehistoric, north-south track joining Hermitage Lane and Blackwell Hollow across the churchyard and Playfield.

In 1283 it was the home of William de Haghindenne, after which there is no documentary record until 1564 when Edward Goodwin bought it from James Catcheford.

John Cranston, who acquired the property by marriage, built a new house on its lands in 1769 and called it East Court [8], a modernised form of Estcots. The original building then became the family's dower house for the older generation and their unmarried daughters.

By 1871 it had reverted to being the home farm house,

and later part of it housed the East Court gardener, until an architect, Albert E. Batzer, bought it in 1926 and restored it as a superior private residence, which it remains to this day, listed grade 2.

The north front of Estcots in 1911 when it was two dwellings and was still known as East Court Farm.

John Cranston, who built East Court in 1769, a London lawyer of Scottish descent, had married a local heiress, Catherine Green. From 1863 to 1903 his descendants let the house to the Rev. Charles Walter Payne Crawfurd, a member of a local family, also of Scottish origin, who served as Chairman of the East Grinstead Local Board 1884-94 and Urban District Council 1894-5. His official chair is in the council chamber and his portrait on the landing.

In 1906 the Cranstons' trustees sold the estate to Ernest Cooper, an accountant from Limpsfield, who gave the building the shape it has now, turning the kitchen into the entrance hall, putting in a new staircase and decorative features, joining the service wing to the main building and constructing the terraces. His portrait too is on the landing.

After his death in 1926 the estate was broken up and the house passed through various private owners until requisitioned for use by the army during the war. In 1946 it was sold with its curtilage to the Urban District Council to be its headquarters while the grounds were bought by the Manor Charitable Trust, set up by Mr Alfred Wagg, a local merchant banker, to be the town's war memorial.

The Rev. C.W.P. Crawfurd (1826-1909), aged about 70, photographed by Fry of Brighton.

On local government re-organisation in 1974 Mid Sussex District Council needed only two rooms but the Town Council, originally leasing two other rooms, gained freehold ownership in 1979. It adapted rooms for public hire, made accommodation available for the Town Museum and let out the top floor. Rooms were later found for meals on wheels, the toy library and other local voluntary groups. The museum, in which portraits of the Cranstons are among the displays, is due to move in 2006 to purpose-built premises in the town centre [71].

The Queen's silver jubilee in 1977 produced on the terraces the 'podium' and a stone marking the line of the Greenwich meridian. The year 2000 was commemorated by an unworked block of stone and a beacon.

In 1986 the Town Council spent £½ million converting the stable block to form the Meridian Hall.

East Court from the south, probably in the 1870s, showing the drive to the original front, now the terraced rear.

THE QUEEN VICTORIA HOSPITAL, Holtye Road

The Queen Victoria Hospital was opened in January 1936 by Princess Helena Victoria at its present location, a few hundred yards from the bottom entrance of East Court. A public meeting in 1931 had initiated moves to replace an inadequate town-centre building with purpose-built premises, for which the London banker Sir Robert Kindersley of Plawhatch near East Grinstead presented the four-and-a-half-acre site.

The building, designed by the architects F.G. Troup and Col. A.C. Denny, had medical facilities on the ground floor and nurses' accommodation on the first floor. A small tower bore a staff encircled by a serpent (a caduceus), a traditional symbol of healing. Superstitions about snakes provoked objections, reinforced when the first deaths occurred.

In 1939 the Ministry of Health designated it an emergency hospital and land was purchased to erect huts for specialisation in maxillo-facial and plastic surgery under Mr Archibald McIndoe. Additional accommodation followed in rather *ad hoc* fashion as responsibilities expanded. Substantial new buildings were the Canadian Wing, with its clocktower, funded in 1942 to acknowledge the increasing number of Canadian Air Force patients by the authorities in that country, and a surgical block fully funded by American sources in 1943.

After the war a nurses' residential block was paid for by Mr Alfred Wagg, Mr and Mrs Douglas Stern funded the assembly hall, and Mr and Mrs Neville Blond financed research laboratories. In 1959 Mr Fred Dart, a bricklayer, councillor and magistrate, his son Eric and some friends voluntarily constructed a schoolroom for the children's ward in their own time. A burns unit followed in 1963, to a novel design, replaced thirty years later in line with new thinking on such treatments. A day hospital was opened in 1990 and a museum created in 1994.

The hospital enjoys an international reputation in several fields and is the only one in Sussex to have consistently achieved three stars since the system came in.

The Queen Victoria Cottage Hospital original buildings when new in 1936.

ST LUKE'S CHURCH, Stone Quarry Estate

East Grinstead's Stone Quarry Estate, on the further side of the hospital, was planned for the Urban District Council on the principles of the 'neighbourhoods' in Crawley new town, each with shops, public house and church to create a sense of community on a human scale.

House-building began in 1948 and was completed four years later, with church services in a temporary hut provided for all community purposes, near where the sub post office now stands.

Fund-raising was undertaken to fulfill the ambition of the vicar of East Grinstead, Dr Golding-Bird, for a permanent church, which would also be the chapel of the hospital, hence the dedication to St Luke, the patron of healing. It was commissioned from the architect E.F. Starling of Redhill and London, to cost not more than £8,000 including fees. About a third of the main space was to be permanently available for church services, with a folding screen so that the remaining area could function as a separate hall. A foyer and study-vestry connected it to the clergy house.

By the time the foundation stone, donated by St Paul's Cathedral, was laid in July 1954 costs had risen to £12,000 and so the building, erected by the

local branch of Y.J. Lovell, and dedicated by Bishop Bell of Chichester the following May, was in debt and lacked the intended small hall, kitchen and boiler-house alongside. They were put up some years later, largely by voluntary labour, as funds permitted.

Stones from the bombed high altar of St Paul's and from Reigate and Brockham (Surrey) churches were incorporated in the east wall. As it was to be the only place of worship in the area, the local Free Churches subscribed £25 towards the furnishings, so covering the cost of the pulpit.

Under its newly-arrived resident curate, the Rev. Edward Finch, St Luke's became the centre of vigorous community activities, secular as well as religious. It never served as the hospital chapel as intended but it still meets the needs of its faithful congregation and local residents in a variety of ways and is a good example of 1950s design and furnishing.

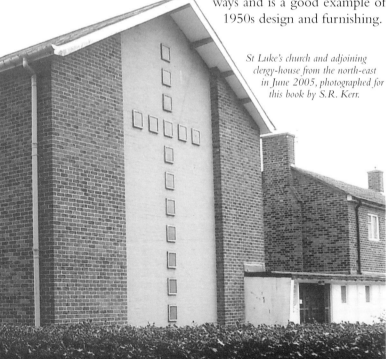

St Luke's church and adjoining clergy-house from the north-east in June 2005, photographed for this book by S.R. Kerr.

For the public house opposite the church [10] E. & H. Kelsey Ltd, the brewers of Flowers' Quality Ales, revived their licence for the *Warwick Arms* which had been at 23 London Road until demolished by the flying bomb that came down on the town centre in 1944. They commissioned Harold Marsh, a Kings Lynn architect and former East Grinstead resident, to design what they proposed to call *The Plume and Garter*, perhaps with the badge of the Royal Sussex Regiment in mind.

The vicar of East Grinstead, Dr Golding-Bird, suggested asking for ideas for a better name, and a former resident, Mr Tim Berry of Newhaven, proposed *The Guinea Pig*. His inspiration was the Guinea Pig Club of seriously burnt airmen who had been patients of the pioneering plastic surgeon Sir Archibald McIndoe at the nearby Queen Victoria Hospital [9]. Accordingly the sign showed a guinea pig in a Spitfire descending in flames, and Sir Archibald performed the opening ceremony in 1957 in the presence of many Guinea Pigs and local dignitaries.

Designed 'in the Georgian tradition', the pub was built by Honour & Sons of East Grinstead in brick with Guildford tiles and surrounded by lawns and cherry trees. To run it Kelseys brought in Fred and Dora Smith from their *Green Man* at Trumpington in Cambridge together with Mr Smith's brother-in-law Bert Bonner.

The Guinea Pig from the west-south-west in June 2005, photographed for this book by S.R. Kerr.

Sir Archibald McIndoe

The only *Guinea Pig* in the world, which like the church looks very much of its period, maintains its links with the club from which it took its name, has supported the hospital's Peanut Ward for children as its charity and has aimed to appeal to all tastes.

Nos 51-53 High Street, by the entrance to the churchyard, was lavishly built in about 1600, with its first floor jettied (overhanging) at both side and front. It replaced an earlier building on the site (originally part of the market place) that formed one end of a first Middle Row before the island development facing it which we know by that name.

Similar buildings, jettied both sides, in the Middle Rows of Edenbridge and Bletchingley may have been market halls, but we have no indication of the original purpose of 51-53 High Street.

We no longer see the jetties because, as frequently happened, floor space was increased by building brick walls supporting them and the upper storey was protected by weather-boarding. The robust roof-structure shows there were once dormer windows. At the rear, however, we can see the stair-tower and faithful modern replacements for the substantial timbers presenting an equally impressive face to the churchyard.

In 1564 the whole stretch as far as today's art shop inclusive counted as three 'cottages', buildings carrying no privileges in the borough, owned by Sir Thomas Sackville and occupied by Thomas Quinnell, about whom and his use of the building, alas, we know nothing.

We know that Richard Plaw, who was here in about 1645, was recorded in 1640 as an innholder, but with no indication of his address, so we cannot conclude that 51-53 was an inn. Thomas Bodle, here in 1662, was a mercer, a dealer in fine fabrics, who issued his own farthing token. By 1669 Robert Mathew, a shoemaker who kept an alehouse, had taken his place.

Thomas Palmer, who came to East Grinstead in 1775 to run the Free School, was here by 1785, acting also as postmaster and stationer and claiming a royal warrant for his pens. Thomas Jackson Palmer, the third generation, added pharmacy. In 1870 the Post Office moved to the London Road corner of the street and in the 1880s Palmer's assistant Walter Henry Dixon took over at 51-53. Dixon's the chemist's, with a branch at the top of Railway Approach, lasted until the 1970s and is still fondly remembered by many.

51-53 High Street, with W.H. Dixon sign, photographed from the west c.1900, attributed to William Page.

THE ROSE AND CROWN, 65-71 High Street

The *Rose and Crown* seen today was built in 1939 by the brewers Ind Coope, who had acquired it three years earlier. It was longer than its predecessor, thanks to taking in the site of a small building and yard to its west, and set a little further back to permit road-widening which, but for the war, would have involved demolishing all the adjoining buildings in front of the churchyard. The previous building seems from photographs to have been a 16th-century timber-framed structure.

The first record of the name is in 1781, simply the *Rose*, but by 1841 it was the *Rose and Crown*. The name probably derives from the arms imputed to the town in the 18th century, the red rose of the Duchy of Lancaster (of which East Grinstead was once part) surmounted by a crown.

In 1887 it was described in the deeds as 'formerly a public house but now and for some years past used as a beerhouse'. A full licence was not applied for again until 1949. The licensee then was Leonard George Gasson, who had been there since 1900, when he had married the widow Kate Florence Edwards, who had run it since 1896. In those days, he recalled, there were no statutory hours, meaning the first drinkers were on the doorstep at 6 a.m. ready to wake him if he overslept and he worked till 11 p.m. There was an ice-plant (a houseleek) on the roof, traditionally thought to protect from lightning, and the landlord was one of those entitled to dry washing on the Playfield at the other end of Church Lane.

In the middle of the 19th century it provided basic accommodation for the poorest classes, as the census returns show, to whom the sisters of St Margaret's frequently took 'custard puddings, gruel and other nourishment'.

In 1940 a 70-foot deep well with running water below the building was sealed and one of the cellars was used as an air-raid shelter for 70 people.

The old Rose and Crown in c. 1937, photographed by Harold Connold.

73-77 HIGH STREET

73-77 High Street in the 1970s and, far end, no. 79, the extension of College View [15].

the property they rented at the other end of Church Lane. Soon the sisters occupied the whole block, using one of the outbuildings as their oratory. Photographs show a sort of verandah-cum-cloister along the front, providing the necessary inter-communication and privacy. The 1861 census records the mother superior and six sisters, two visitors, one boarder, two servants and 33 orphans aged from 3 to 16. In 1870 the sisters moved into purpose-built premises of their own, now called the Old Convent [74], though they used this block for a little longer.

In 1881 Francis Moore Wilcox established a saddler's business on the corner which continued until the mid-1950s. George Read, furniture dealer, was next door but soon moved to London Road.

In about 1905 Thomas Taylor, who had set up a cycle and motor business with William King in 1893, moved into the middle shop, trading alone. In 1921 he sold to Harold John Pearson, whose son Norman took over in 1949 and still, at the time of writing, runs it as a traditional cycle-dealers. With its original functional gas-lighting and principled stance in the face of contemporary trends and consumerism, it is one of those prized features that prevent East Grinstead from being just like any other town.

The easternmost shop became a ladies' hairdressers soon after the First World War and, through many changes of name and ownership, so continues into the 21st century.

Nos 73-77 High Street and the stylistically similar building in Church Lane, opposite the *Rose and Crown* [13], were built in the mid-1850s for George Felton, a currier (dresser of leather) who was already carrying on business on the site. They seem to be the town's first block of shops of modern type with living accommodation over.

In 1858 Felton's housekeeper persuaded him to let the vacant corner house to the sisters of St Margaret's, whose good work she had seen and whose temporary unpopularity meant they had to vacate

COLLEGE VIEW, 81 High Street

From the street College View is a typically symmetrical and attractive Regency house. From the side or rear it is obvious that it is a much earlier building, converted at the front when the road was lowered for laying out Lewes Road on its present line in 1826.

The late Peter Gray of the Wealden Buildings Study Group surveyed College View in 1998 and found it originated as part of a non-domestic timber-framed range built on the street in about 1500. The ground floor accommodation was nine feet high. A stone-fronted basement survives but at some point the easternmost part of the original structure was demolished.

This section of the High Street was not within the borough and no records survive to throw light on College View's original purpose.

Early in the 17th century a timber-framed domestic extension was created at its rear. In the mid-19th century a single-storey addition was built on its western side, soon extended onto the pavement and later given an upper storey. It is currently an undertaker's, no.79 High Street.

On the other side of College View the original northern edge of the High Street survives as the path in front of Sackville College.

In the first half of the 19th century College View housed the Morris family's leather-cutting and dressing business. This side of the High Street from Church Lane eastwards had already been associated with leather-working of all kinds from at least 1546, and so continued at no.73 until living memory. Thomas Morris, a currier (leather-dresser) and spirit merchant, committed suicide in 1845 but his widow Jane kept on the wine and spirit business until her death two decades later, after which her son James ran it for about another 16 years. College View then became a private residence, eventually listed grade 2.

College View in 1986, photographed by Miss R.M. Willatts.

SACKVILLE COLLEGE

Impressively dominating the eastern approach to the town, Sackville College is one of only four grade 1 listed buildings in East Grinstead, rated by the architectural historian Alec Clifton-Taylor one of his hundred favourite buildings in the whole country.

It is a college in the sense of a community of people living a regulated common life, in this case an almshouse, founded by Robert Sackville, 2nd Earl of Dorset in 1608, but also including prestigious accommodation for his family whenever county business required attendance in East Grinstead or when travelling to and from London and their country seats. The plan, a quadrangle with chapel and hall, resembles that of an Oxford or Cambridge college but on a homelier scale.

Today it fulfills the modern equivalent of its original purpose as a kind of sheltered housing, with the Warden and his family living

Sackville College from the south-east in 1890.

J.M. Neale and his family at their door in the quadrangle in 1855 (possibly by Joseph Cundall).

Interior of the hall, mid-20th century (Harold Connold).

in the Earl's quarters, while Earl De La Warr, descended through marriage from the Sackvilles, is the patron. It is open to the public in the summer months.

The most famous Warden was the Rev. John Mason Neale, best known today for his hymns and carols and for founding here the Society of St Margaret, one of the first orders of nuns in the Church of England, in 1854. When he arrived in 1846 the College was in a poor state of repair. He had it thoroughly renovated by the leading architect William Butterfield, including extending and re-ordering the chapel and creating the wellhouse.

WOODBURY HOUSE, Lewes Road

The Woodbury Hotel in the early 1960s, before being extended on the left, photographed by Malcolm Powell and published by him as a postcard.

Woodbury, as it was originally called, on the left side of Lewes Road as it leaves the town, at the junction with Woodbury Avenue, to which it gives name, was built in 1895. The earliest resident I can name is Henry Edmund Mathews, in 1899, an architect and probably its designer. His work in East Grinstead included a house in Portland Road in 1896, the Masonic Temple in St James's Road in 1898, and the west door of the parish church, where he was a churchwarden, in 1910. His wife, Florence, had one of the first motor cars in East Grinstead, a 6¼ horsepower Mars. Around the start of the First World War the Mathews moved out but the practice continued in London Road until the 1930s as Mathews, Son & Ridley.

For nearly half a century Woodbury continued as a private house, at one point apparently divided into flats, but by 1963 it had become a 'countryhouse type hotel' for long- or short-term residential stays, bed and breakfast or meals for non-residents. By 1971 it was advertising 'all rooms with basins – some with bathrooms'. There were 14 bedrooms in 1978, at from £5 per night single, £10 double, including service charge but not V.A.T.

Around that time a regular lunch-guest, accompanied by his bull terrier, was Colonel Maurice Buckmaster, who had led the French section of the Special Operations Executive through most of the Second World War. In 1987 the owners, Michael and Jane Medforth, persuaded him to open a new dining room named in his honour. He had already lent his name to streets in France. After his death in 1992 memories faded, the hotel changed hands and his name was dropped, but amends were made in 2001 with the Buckmaster bistro and bar.

There were plans for expansion but they foundered on the difficulty of filling the existing rooms and so in 2002 it was decided to close the hotel and convert it to flats, a lengthy operation amounting almost to rebuilding.

Former patrons still miss the good service, good food and reasonable prices that it offered while an hotel.

THE GATE-LODGES, BARTON ST MARY, Lewes Road

The gate-lodges to Barton St Mary, opposite the mouth of Woodbury Avenue, and the house which they guard were designed by Sir Edward Landseer Lutyens for George Munro Miller in 1906. Nothing has yet been discovered about Miller, nor any explanation of the name he chose for his house.

Lutyens did a good deal of work in the East Grinstead area, mostly, like Barton St Mary, not visible from public roads. He was a perfectionist, attending minutely to detail and employing the traditional materials and some of the idioms of each locality yet always originally and uniquely. Thus Barton St Mary is approached between two identical gate-lodges spanning the drive, colour-washed brick on the lower storey, tile-hung above. The inner walls of the carriageway are partly half-timbered and partly lined with the small bricks Lutyens specially ordered for the house. It is typical of Lutyens that these walls are not parallel to each other but slightly narrowing the space between them towards the gates from either end. The dormers and tall chimney-stacks are typical of his work also.

In 1962 the lodges and house were listed grade 2, not qualifying for 2* or 1 because the house had been altered too much.

The gate-lodges photographed in 1978 by L. & M. Gayton.

POYNDERS, 92 High Street

Poynders in 1975, photographed for the East Grinstead Society's photographic record of every building in the original High Street conservation area.

In a style strongly influenced by the Arts and Crafts movement it was built of good quality local materials with a solid oak front door, interesting reproduction medieval brickwork and ornamental chimneys. Dressed sandstone was used for window openings, two south-facing bays faced with weather-tiling, and a loggia accessed through a fine sandstone and glass weather-screen. There are southerly views to Ashdown Forest and Weir Wood reservoir.

Dr Poynder was still living there in 1938, though his association with the Queen Victoria Hospital had ended 12 years earlier, but towards the end of the war it was vacant. Suggestions were made for acquiring the house, by now called Poynders, for a maternity hospital, a museum or a replacement vicarage.

Where Lewes Road ends and the High Street begins, on the same side of the road as Barton St Mary, stands Poynders, designed by E. Turner for Dr Frederick Cecil Poynder, who had arrived in East Grinstead early in 1900 and taken over the practice of Dr Wright-Edwards of Sackville House [24]. Despite the date 1900 on the keystone of the arch over the porch, the building does not appear in the 1901 census, which records Dr Poynder as a London-born 38-year-old bachelor living at Dorset House [26]. An article about it in the 21 August 1903 issue of the journal *The Architect* probably indicates the date by which it had been completed.

In the early 1950s the surveyors R.H. & R.W. Clutton moved into it from Old Stone House [40], adapted the whole building for offices and built a two-storey westward extension to house a member of staff.

Later the orchard was sold, to be the site of Sackville Court, from the entrance to whose drive in Fairfield Road alongside Poynders one can obtain a good view of the rear of the building.

Cluttons, whose business is 260 years old but who did not come to East Grinstead until shortly before the Second World War, still use the house, of which they are rightly proud.

THE OLD LOCK-UP, 90 High Street

When the East Sussex police force was set up in 1840, East Grinstead was one of the places to which a constable was allocated. James Flanagan, P.C. no. 2, was appointed in 1841, but there was no police building in the town so he had to live in lodgings. Because the existing lock-up, used by the unpaid parish constable, had no windows, Flanagan had to walk those he arrested 20 miles to Lewes, after first taking them to a magistrate.

In 1841 the first purpose-built police-houses with cells attached were ordered, and soon this one was constructed at the end of East Grinstead High Street, adjoining numbers 86-88. From the street one can see the diamond-shaped cell window, set high up to provide light but prevent any contact with the world outside. One can also see a different type of brickwork on the first floor, suggesting it was originally a one-storey structure.

In 1860 a fully appointed police station for a larger force was built in West Street (demolished in 1965) but the original building continued to be a policeman's house for a while. Later it was sold and became a private house. The name, the Old Lock-Up, seems to be very recent. It is in the conservation area and listed grade 2.

The Old Lock-Up, drawn by the late Kenneth Peters in the mid-1980s for its then owner, the late Ann Standen, widow of Henry Standen, for many years the editor of the Guinea Pigs' magazine.

86-88 HIGH STREET

Although two separate dwellings with contrasting frontages, 86-88 is a single building under one roof, in fact a 15th-century hall-house with massive internal timbering.

It is an addition to the original lay-out of the town. Unlike the other burgage tenements it never had a portland, an associated strip of land to its rear, and it is separated from the rest by what is now merely an access to garages. In the 16th century that was the lane to Washingwell or Washwell Common, the public area for the women of the borough to do their laundry in the flowing water of what is now a tiny stream along the bottom of the portlands into the grounds of Great House Court.

In 1564, in our first documentary reference, this building was owned and occupied by John Payne, together with its neighbours Porch House and Cromwell House [22 and 23]. The family still held the whole stretch in 1683.

We do not know who actually lived there and what they did until 1790, when the church rate book records George Ellis, who with William Ellis (presumably his son) appears in our first directory,

86-88 High Street in 1975, photographed for the East Grinstead Society's photographic record of every building in the original High Street conservation area.

in 1794, as poulterers and higlers. That means they bred poultry and bought other people's surplus chickens and eggs to sell at markets. By 1811 William Ellis was also a currier, a dresser of leather. His successor by 1823, George Langridge, was a shoemaker who by 1828 had added fishmongering.

Lowering the street level in 1826 for the present line of Lewes Road explains the number of steps at the doors. A tile inscribed by its maker 'Edward Payne, June 10, 1842' was found at no.88 during 20th-century building operations. The division of the house had taken place by 1861, after which the occupants and their occupations changed increasingly rapidly, with residential use taking over as the town's commercial centre was steadily drawn down London Road.

In the second half of the 20th century no.88 was given the name Windsor Cottage – I do not know why – and the whole structure was listed grade 2.

PORCH HOUSE, 82-84 High Street

From the street there is no sign of the porch that gave this house its modern name, first recorded in 1925. It was added in the 17th century, at the rear, to what seems to have been at first the only entrance, accessed from the space separating it from nos 86-88. At the same time a detached privy, also of local sandstone, was constructed in the grounds.

The house itself dates from the later 16th century and is faced and roofed with local stone but at the side the timber-framing with brick infill can still be seen. Careful inspection of the façade reveals at least one stone set up on end rather than horizontally as it should have been. Comparison with early photographs, such as those reproduced here and with the next entry, shows that by the mid-19th century several windows had been blocked up, but a street-door was created around the turn of the century. The windows were unblocked and a stone with the new name was put over the front door in the mid-1920s when the house was acquired by the father of the artist Geoffrey Webb, who lived further along at Sackville House [24].

The first written record is in 1564, when it was owned and occupied by John Payne along with the houses either side. The Paynes were by then of considerable importance in East Grinstead and continued to hold these properties until they were acquired by the Sackvilles.

As far as one can tell, they were let out for residential rather than commercial use. At the end of the 18th century Thomas Fulcher, a surgeon and man-midwife, lived in Porch House, followed in the 19th by William Avery, a butcher and brickmaker.

No old name is known for Porch House, which constitutes one of the burgages dating from the laying-out of the town in the early 13th century, the properties whose owners ran the town and enjoyed certain privileges within it. The associated portland (literally 'town land'), a long strip running back some 200 yards, still retains its original boundaries and is thus one of the oldest surviving features of the town. For this reason, permission has never been given for it to be built upon. Even so, a few years ago the asking price for this grade 2 building was £1 million.

The porch of Porch House in 1903.

CROMWELL HOUSE, 78 High Street

A late 16th-century structure that seems always to have been shared between them, containing the street-doors of both until one was created in Porch House, joins that building to Cromwell House, the most impressive timber-framed building in East Grinstead High Street. Cromwell House soars above its neighbours to demonstrate the wealth and status of its builders, Edward and Anne Payne, whose initials and the date 1599 were carved on the main fireplace. A pane of coloured glass bore the date 1598. The family had made money from the iron industry and by 1564 owned and occupied not only the predecessor of the house we see today but also all the buildings to its east. These remained the property of the Paynes until at least the end of the 17th century.

The name Cromwell House has not been found before 1887, given, it has been suggested, because Oliver Cromwell was born in 1599. At the end of the 18th century it was known as the Great House and was the home of Charles Smith, a builder and auctioneer.

In the late 1870s two dormer windows were created in the roof and by the turn of the century the east gable had been hung with tiles. In August 1913 the fireplace and all the oak panelling were removed

to London, 'spoliation' that prompted a call for the Urban District Council to acquire the house for a museum and library. Nothing came of this suggestion, but wall-paintings, including a hunting scene, were uncovered, probably part of the original decoration.

On the night of 9 December 1928, when no-one was at home, Cromwell House caught fire and only the shell remained standing. It was carefully rebuilt as before, except that the gables were exposed again and three dormer windows were provided. It is now listed grade 2.

The fronts of Porch House (far left), no.80, Cromwell House and their neighbours photographed by William Harding c.1864 (as reproduced by his son Arthur as a postcard in the early 20th century).

SACKVILLE HOUSE, 70 High Street

Anyone who has ever fantasised about living in a timber-framed house in East Grinstead High Street has the possibility of doing so – briefly – in Sackville House, next but one after Cromwell House. Its last owner as a private home, Mrs Ursula Honess, to prevent any risk of its being spoilt, left it to the Landmark Trust, an independent charity that takes over historic properties to let for self-catering holidays. The trust, which inherited Sackville House in 1995, researches their histories and conserves them to the highest standards.

The Wealden Buildings Study Group has dated Sackville House, originally a three-bay two-storied structure with integral access to the rear, where stood a detached kitchen, to about 1525. In about 1574, apparently as part of conversion to a short-lived inn called the *Lion*, a chimney and cellar were inserted and the kitchen connected to the rest of the building. In the early 18th century the roof was rebuilt and dormer windows were put in.

The earliest documentary evidence is from 1564, when Sackville House counted as one burgage and Andrew Ledger was the owner-occupier. It continued in the Ledger family until the late 17th century and was occupied in about 1645 by John Allen, a mercer. By the late 18th century the Sackvilles had acquired it and John Collins, an attorney (solicitor), was living there. He was followed by his son, also John, and his grandson, Miles Bailey Collins, both surgeons. Later a bootmaker lived there and a builder used the yard, but in 1877, at the start of his career, Dr P.E. Wallis lodged there – according to a daughter 'in a damp room with swarms of lice over the gateway'.

Geoffrey Webb (1879-1954)

In 1919 the house was acquired and cared for by Mrs Honess's father, the artist Geoffrey Webb, who raised the roof level in order to use the attic as his studio. He exposed the timber-framing and created a grille in the gate so that passers-by could see the magnificent view of Ashdown Forest. There are examples of his stained glass in Felbridge church and St Mary's, East Grinstead [59]. The originals of some posters he painted are on show in the Town Museum.

The name Sackville House has not been found before 1885, preserving the link soon after that family had disposed of it.

Sackville House is listed grade 2 and occasionally opened to the public for a day, including the 630-foot long portland, which becomes less formal as the ground falls away, until one seems to be in the heart of the countryside.

Sackville House (no later than c. 1920).

AMHERST HOUSE, 68 High Street

Amherst House, adjoining Sackville House, is the third-oldest building in East Grinstead High Street, tree-ring dated to summer 1369 and spring 1370. Into the standard 33-foot wide plot it squeezes both a narrow two-bay open hall and a floored-over end bay.

In the 15th century it was given by Thomas Ryngare to John Brether, vicar of East Grinstead, by whom in turn it was bequeathed in 1500 to the Fraternity of St Katherine. The fraternity, a devotional and philanthropic organisation connected with the parish church, was to rent it out to generate income for its good works. When the fraternity was dissolved in 1548 the house was known as Ryngars after its former owner. It was soon acquired by the Sackvilles, who sold it before the end of the century but had obtained it again two centuries later, for by then the parliamentary vote it carried had made it a valuable possession. In 1841 Earl De La Warr was the owner and John Moon, a tailor and milkman, the tenant. His family remained there for almost another hundred years.

In 1938 a new owner incorporated no.66 into no.68, extended it at the rear, exposed the framing, including the curious balustering over the front door, and named it Amherst House, unaware of its history, including the ancient name, which had long fallen out of use. The inspiration was the fact that the last Duke of Dorset's sister, Mary, was Countess Amherst. In the light of what we now know, his other sister, Elizabeth Countess De La Warr, would have been a more appropriate figure.

The work in 1938 gave the first opportunity for R.T. Mason, who pioneered the study of local timber-framed structures, to investigate the building and publish an illustrated account of it, along with others in our High Street.

Amherst House (no later than c.1920).

DORSET HOUSE, 62-64 High Street

With its elegant Queen Anne façade, Dorset House is one of the most impressive buildings on our High Street, obviously much younger than most of its neighbours. Even so, the interior retains vestiges of the timber-framed structure that preceded it.

The precise year of its completion is visible on a rainwater head, 1705, together with the initials of those responsible, Thomas and Katherine James. They had acquired the property by 1695 and undoubtedly wanted a fine town house to complement their country home at Cowden. Their son, also Thomas, succeeded them, but soon after becoming vicar of East Grinstead in 1746 he leased it out, and in 1770 the Sackvilles acquired it for the sake of the vote it carried.

Under their ownership it was occupied by a series of lawyers until at least 1881. Soon after that it became a boarding house. Dr William Henry Marshall owned and occupied it from 1925 until 1947 when he sold it to Tamplins, the brewers, who made it an annexe of their *Dorset Arms* hotel next door. For a while, after the hotel ceased to offer accommodation in about 1980, it was empty and deteriorating but then Grand Metropolitan Estates Ltd acquired it for conversion to offices. The building was extended sympathetically at the rear and meticulously restored in 1988, with as much retention or re-use of the original materials as possible.

The name Dorset House has not been traced before 1885, and was given to recognise ownership by the Sackvilles as Earls and later Dukes of Dorset until they disposed of their High Street properties in the 1870s and 80s.

Little is known about the pre-1705 building, which is first recorded in 1564 when Andrew Cole was the owner and Thomas Wright the tenant. Wright was a shoemaker who was in trouble in 1577 for feeding pigs in the street. A hundred years later another shoemaker, and also alehouse-keeper, Robert Mathew, lived there.

Dorset House is listed grade 2.

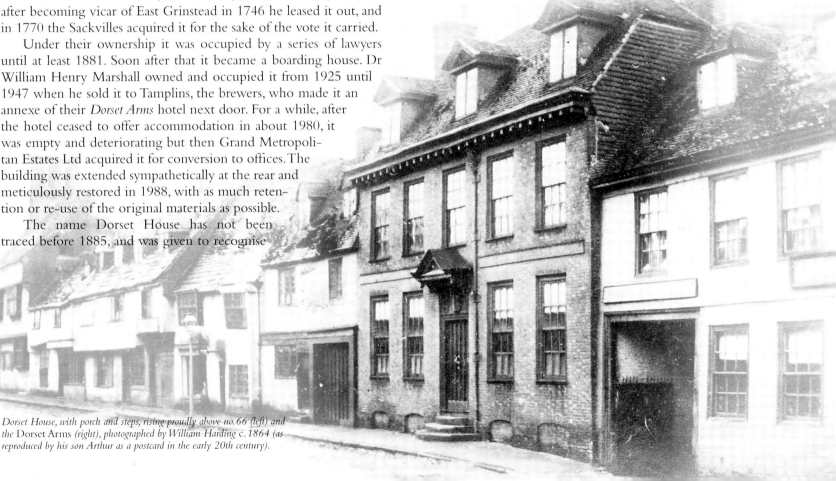

Dorset House, with porch and steps, rising proudly above no. 66 (left) and the Dorset Arms (right), photographed by William Harding c. 1864 (as reproduced by his son Arthur as a postcard in the early 20th century).

THE DORSET ARMS, 58 High Street

The name of the *Dorset Arms*, adjoining Dorset House, is little more than 150 years old and the present building not much more than 300, but its history can be traced back to 1564, when John Duffield was owner and occupier.

We do not know its name and function then, but by 1605 it was a tavern, the *Ounce and Ivy Bush*. Eighteenth-century deeds show that its previous name was the *New Inn*. In 1614 when Henry Baldwin applied for a wine licence it was the *Cat*, a name which persisted until at least 1776.

A tavern was a superior establishment, licensed to sell wine and indicated as such by an ivy bush outside. Ounces, a kind of wild cat, are the supporters of the coat of arms of the Sackvilles, Earls and later Dukes of Dorset, so all these names amount to the same thing, astute recognition of the growing dominance of that family in and around East Grinstead well before it became the inn's owners in the 18th century.

The brickwork at the junction with Dorset House, dated 1705, shows that the present-day *Dorset Arms* is the older of the two, though not by much. Later additions and alterations have made more precise dating impossible.

In 1650 Thomas Page of the *Cat* issued farthing tokens, the oldest dated examples in Sussex, one of which is displayed in the Town Museum. A hundred years later it had become a coaching inn, the midday halt on the London-Lewes-Brighton route. After another century and a half it made a point of catering for motorists. As one of East Grinstead's two principal inns throughout the 19th century the *Dorset Arms* hosted balls, public meetings, courts of law and friendly societies as well as providing food, drink and accommodation at the upper end of the range.

In the mid-1990s it closed and looked like following its historic rival the *Crown* [47] into extinction, but it was bought and saved. It is listed grade 2.

The Dorset Arms *in 1928, still 'for families and gentlemen'.*

Middle Row from the church tower in the first decade of the 20th century, with re-roofing of Wilmington House [29] underway in the background.

When East Grinstead High Street was first laid out, in the early 13th century, it would have been roughly the same width throughout, with the area in front of the church serving as the market place. As time went on, more substantial structures than market stalls were required, and so in about 1400 permanent buildings began to be put up along the front of the churchyard, leaving only a footpath between. Increasing trade then required even more commercial buildings, and so a second row was created along the centre of the road, our Middle Row.

At first its buildings were single rooms, about 15 feet square, but subsequently extended upwards and at the rear. Buildings of that sort of size survive today in front of the churchyard and in Middle Row, some of them datable to the 15th century on structural evidence. There is documentary evidence of the same date giving names of some of the townsmen who had them built, though unfortunately we cannot identify individual buildings in the written records.

The earliest were shambles, i.e. butchers' slaughterhouses. By 1564 Middle Row also contained a stable associated with the *Crown* inn, a currying house (where leather is dressed and coloured after tanning) and a workshop of some other kind. There is no evidence that Middle Row ever stretched further than it does today.

By the 1930s Middle Row, unstudied and unappreciated, was perceived as an obstruction best swept away for the sake of motor vehicles travelling on the London-Eastbourne road. The war prevented any such action but the first list of buildings of historical and architectural interest, in August 1946, suggested the High Street 'might be greatly improved' by removing it completely, an opinion shared by E. W. Young, a writer brought up in the town some seventy years earlier.

By 1972, however, when the list was revised, Middle Row's contribution to the street scene was recognised and it was listed grade 2. The opening of the relief road in 1978 ended its unenviable distinction of being the narrowest and therefore the most congested point on the whole length of the A22.

Middle Row, being opposite the church, is a convenient point at which to end or begin a perambulation.

In 1939 Wilmington House, behind Middle Row on the corner of Portland Road, was derelict and for sale as building materials when a lady named Lydia Craven fell in love with it, bought it, restored it and privately published an illustrated booklet about it.

Some of her conclusions about the structural history can no longer be sustained but we can confidently claim the western half as one of the oldest buildings in the town, an early 14th-century hall-house which has, alas, been unable to provide samples adequate for precise tree-ring dating. The jetty, projecting the first-floor chamber forward, has its joists laid untypically, and perhaps experimentally, parallel to the street rather than at right-angles. In the 16th century a wide access to the rear was created through the hall, so enabling us to see the fine moulded beam that graced its more important end, now suffering from exposure to the elements.

The eastern half may be of late 17th- or early 18th-century origin but was partly rebuilt in modern times, as were the structures at the rear.

Each half occupies one of the burgage plots dating from the original laying-out of the town, including a portland, hence the name given to the road alongside when created in the early 1890s.

The name Wilmington House, which has not been found before 1885, commemorates the ownership of the eastern half by Spencer Compton, who was one of East Grinstead's M.P.s 1713-22 and created Earl of Wilmington in 1730. When the bookshop set up here by Lydia Craven migrated across the High Street to nos 55-57 in the 1950s it took the name Wilmington with it.

The access created through the building, showing the beam mentioned below on the left and part of Middle Row in the background (drawn by F. Smart in 1940 for Lydia Craven's booklet).

No earlier name is known for the building, which over the centuries has seen a variety of tenants with varied occupations and which, thanks to Lydia Craven, is deservedly listed grade 2.

34-40 HIGH STREET

Nos 34-40 High Street, impressively facing across the western end of Middle Row, consists of a hall-house with an integral through-passage as part of the original structure and, at the western end, a building constructed, unusually, end-on to the street. The eastern part (nos 36-40), tree-ring dated to 1351-2, is probably the oldest building in the town. The western part (no.34), which was not able to be tree-ring dated but is attributed to *c*.1410-20 on other grounds, seems to have been an important, perhaps civic, building, and is of particularly notable quality. Since the whole structure is a shop, the public can see some of the original features inside.

A feature that has been lost, once carved in the stone vault of a cellar at the rear, is the coat of arms acquired in 1272 by the Dallingridge family, who died out locally in 1469. This suggests they had something to do with the construction and use of the building, but we do not know its original purpose, nor its use when first recorded in a written document, a survey of the borough in 1564, when John Leedes was the owner and John Wynsor the tenant and it counted as two burgages with 11 portlands.

In the 16th and 17th centuries, however, it is well recorded as an inn, the *Lion* or *Red Lion*. In the 19th the eastern part was an ironmonger's, the western a plumber's and later also a builder's. Its current use, a tailor's and outfitter's, was established in 1896 by George Herbert Broadley from Bromley. After a spell as a music shop, the western part was incorporated in the 1950s. The present shop-front, hand-crafted in oak and held together in the traditional way with wooden pegs, was installed across the whole building in 1966. Today it is still run by the Broadley family, one of our oldest surviving family businesses and so itself as much part of the character of East Grinstead as the fine grade 2 listed building in which the family take such pride.

34-40 High Street in 1986, photographed by Miss R.M.Willatts.

30-32 HIGH STREET

It replaced a fine building, attributed to about 1480, with a jettied upper storey, heavy and handsome joisting and joinery, a noble moulded fascia beam and some fragments of wall-painting. The rear portion was older.

Little of this had been discovered when in 1967 the owners, the pharmacists Savory and Moore, having been refused permission to demolish in 1963, applied again. The Urban District Council again resisted but could not find adequate grounds to dismiss an appeal. The building was not listed, merely on the then 'supplementary list', its structure having been only superficially investigated, and the High Street still comparatively unstudied and not yet a conservation area. Public opinion was generally against, but there was no organisation to present a case for opposition within the constraints of planning law. Demolition therefore began in January 1968, alerting people to the potential risk to the rest of the street.

In response the East Grinstead Society was formed, to safeguard the town's historic buildings, if necessary by fighting appeals against planning decisions. The society's meetings and publications, particularly a report on the High Street in 1969, began to spread understanding and appreciation of East Grinstead's distinctive heritage, not least among those in authority. At the same time awareness was growing nationally of the importance of historic buildings and their environments, leading to the creation of conservation areas and the listing of other properties than the most outstanding. No such fate has threatened East Grinstead High Street since.

Next to Broadleys stands a building of special significance in the history of East Grinstead, built in 1968 as an unremarkable shop with standard plate-glass frontage on the ground floor and, as a concession to its neighbours, vertical timber strips on the first-floor façade, and a roof of Horsham stone.

30-32 High Street shortly before demolition, photographed by P.D. Wood from his office window in 29 High Street.

TUDOR HOUSE, 22-24 High Street

The name Tudor House is of 20th-century origin, given before timber-framed buildings had been properly studied. In fact the building was already there when the Tudors came to power, a fine mid-15th-century hall-house of the Wealden type, still structurally almost intact. Unfortunately not enough evidence could be found for it to be scientifically dated during the East Grinstead Society's tree-ring dating survey.

No earlier name is known and there is no documentary record before 1564 when it was owned and occupied by Edward Goodwin. Indeed there are few documentary references to it at all, compared to other buildings in our High Street, and little is known of the uses to which it was put before the mid-19th century.

In 1861 it was shared between Elizabeth Pace, a cooper, and John Tooth, a plumber and painter. He eventually acquired the whole building, creating a shop with old panelling from elsewhere and new Tudoresque ornamentation. He also idiosyncratically added cork-oak bark to the façade. Starting with Christmas cards, his son Frederick converted the business to a stationer's and bookseller's together with his younger brother Edwin. Mr and Mrs Edwin Tooth, by then in their 80s, were killed in July 1943 when a bomb struck their house in the grounds behind. The

Tudor House (Edwin Tooth's shop) in the 1930s, with part of nos 30-32 (H.S. Martin) far left.

ceiling of Tudor House was damaged but not the walls, and no serious damage was done in 1995 when a fire broke out on the first floor.

In 1991 a new owner replaced general stationery with coffee and extended the shop area upstairs. Tudor House is thus one of the few buildings in the town where we can admire almost the whole interior at our leisure. It is listed grade 2.

THE JUBILEE DRINKING FOUNTAIN

To celebrate Queen Victoria's golden jubilee in 1887 the Rev. C.W. Payne Crawfurd offered to have a public drinking fountain constructed in the High Street at his own expense. He had been born at Saint Hill [79] in 1826 but was now a private resident at East Court [8].

The design, by the vicar of East Grinstead, the Rev. D.Y. Blakiston, who had originally trained as an artist, echoes architectural features of Sackville College [16]. It is constructed of yellow York stone with a red Mansfield stone roof, originally topped by a carving of the feathers from the town's seal of arms of 1572. The water spouted, when a button was pushed, from the mouths of two bronze dolphins with tails entwined, to which metal cups were attached by chains. The fountain was constructed by James Charlwood's building firm and the mason's work was executed by his employee James Jenner, whose descendants still live in the town.

At daybreak on jubilee day, however, 21 June, when the fountain was to be officially handed over, it was found to have been freely sprinkled with boiled tar. The reason must have been Crawfurd's withdrawal of support from the town band the previous month on account of its unauthorised participation in the spontaneous popular celebrations of the verdict that the former workhouse site was parish property.

Some eighty or more years later the finial disappeared, apparently unnoticed, to be followed equally unobtrusively by the dolphins in the late 1970s. Mid Sussex District Council provided rather crude concrete replacements for both but they too were removed without record. By then the fountain had been listed grade 2.

For the centenary of their movement in 2005, however, East Grinstead's two rotary clubs in partnership with the Town Council restored the stonework and commissioned a replacement finial in the original stone but with no intention of re-instating the water supply. Completion of the work was marked by a plaque on the ground and a short ceremony on 17 June 2005.

The fountain on 8 August 1975, with the finial gone but the dolphins still in place, photographed by C.W. Goolden.

10-14 HIGH STREET

10-14 High Street, behind and between the central and right-hand trees in June 2005, photographed for this book by S.R. Kerr.

For over 200 years, 10-14 High Street, between the fountain and the war memorial, was an inn, the *Bull*. The first reference to it by name is in 1619, when Edward Drewe bequeathed it to his wife with 20 shillings to its occupant, John Butchinge, in consideration of his having built a chimney at his own expense. It was probably already so used in 1564, when George Partriche was owner and occupier, for he appears as a baker from 1573 to 88, a tippler (seller of drink) in 1578 and an unlicensed alehouse-keeper in 1594-5.

The present timber-framed building dates from the mid-17th century, apparently designed for business on the ground floor and living accommodation above.

John Bodle kept an alehouse here in 1662. In 1710 Thomas Bodle sold it to Edward Head and Francis Greene, who undoubtedly wanted to secure for the Earl of Dorset the parliamentary vote it carried. At the 1715 election Greene arranged a treat at the *Bull* on behalf of the Earl's candidate Lord Shannon, for which the bill survives, together with another arranged by Henry Johnson, both receipted by Edmund Chapman the landlord.

In 1784 smugglers entered the stable and retook two horses that the excise officer had just seized laden with tea, which he had already removed to his house. By then Lord Sackville was the owner and Elizabeth Turley, a widow, was running the *Bull*.

It ceased being an inn in about 1800, a consequence of East Grinstead's loss of through traffic to the direct London-Brighton road. For most of the ensuing century the eastern part, no.10, was a butcher's, and the western, nos 12-14, had various retail uses. In 1877 Edward Gatland, the butcher, bought the whole property from Earl De La Warr's trustees. In 1918 the tailor Alec Johnson moved into no.10 when his premises at the end of Middle Row were rebuilt as a bank. Ann Dolphin, ladies' outfitter, in no.10 at the time of writing, is in direct line from that business. The building is listed grade 2.

THE WAR MEMORIAL

Our memorial was designed and made by the sculptor Ernest G. Gillick of Chelsea, who was also responsible for some of the statuary on the front of the Victoria and Albert Museum, and erected by the local masons Messrs Jenner and Grynyer. It consists of a hexagonal shaft of Clipsham stone, 25 feet high, surmounted by a gilt bronze cross and standing on a circular base of York stone 12 feet in diameter with small retaining walls of local sandstone. Its colours and proportions were designed to be in harmony with the old buildings in the High Street. On a panel facing the street is the town's 1572 seal of arms – five feathers – and this inscription: 'In gratitude to the men of East Grinstead who gave their lives for their country during the Great War of 1914-18. This monument is erected by the inhabitants that future generations may value the freedom for which they died and that their names may be kept in honoured memory.' Panels on the other five faces list 194 townsmen and one man with local connections who lost their lives serving in that war.

Despite hard-line Protestant objections to the cross, the memorial was unveiled in an inter-denominational ceremony on Sunday 23 July 1922 by Admiral of the Fleet Sir Charles Madden, commander-in-chief of the Atlantic fleet and then living at Herontye [93]. He let fall the union flag normally flown from the church tower and the white ensign which flew at the masthead of the British ship to which the German fleet had surrendered. He pointed out that some 1,000 of East Grinstead's population of about 7,000 had served in the war.

The memorial was entrusted to the Urban District Council and is now the responsibility of the Town Council and the scene of an impressive ceremony every Remembrance Sunday.

The Second World War is commemorated by a memorial at East Court [8]. Local residents who lost their lives in subsequent conflicts are honoured, though not by name, on a plaque added to the High Street memorial a few years ago.

The war memorial when new in 1923.

4 HIGH STREET

This building, just beyond and behind the war memorial, was constructed as what is termed a half-Wealden house, a two-bay open-hall with a floored end-bay whose upper storey projected forward. The main structure has been tree-ring dated to 1452, the same decade as several other buildings in our High Street and, it is being found, in other towns across the country. The insertion of the attic over the hall was dated to 1630.

The earliest written record is in 1564, when it was one of several properties owned by John Payne and its tenant was Thomas Underhill, a butcher. A deed of 1572 reveals that its name then was Gaynesfords, derived from a former owner. The Gaynesford family acquired property in Crowhurst and Dormans Land and built Old Surrey Hall in the 15th century, so they were almost certainly responsible for constructing this building as a nearby townhouse in keeping with their status.

Although we know who lived here at several dates in the 17th and 18th centuries, we do not know what their occupations were. By 1811, however, the tenant was Stephen Scott, a butcher, and it continued to be a butcher's right up to the First World War. The occupant in 1894, Albert Ellis, objected to the erection of a wall and fence on the slope in front, for it would then no longer be possible for carts to come right up to the door. By 1923 it had become Flomarie's, serving dainty teas, a use which continued until at least 1953.

The building was listed grade 2 in 1946. By then the residential accommodation above the shop was known as the Burgher's House, disregarding the fact that the terms used in this town, and I believe in the whole country, were burgageholder or burgess. Burghers began at Calais!

4 High Street towards the end of the 20th century.

CONSTITUTIONAL BUILDINGS

This imposing block at the western end of the High Street fronting London Road was built in 1893 for the Constitutional Club, the Conservative social club for gentlemen. The design was the result of a competition with a prize of five guineas but the name of the winning architect seems unrecorded. Until 1930 the first floor was approached by an external stairway and balcony, from which election results were proclaimed. Then the club moved out, the steps were demolished and the building was converted to a tearoom and other business uses.

Previously the site had been occupied by four brick cottages, known as the Round Houses or West Buildings, put up in the 18th century and the only known examples of back-to-back building in the town. When the road was lowered in 1828, for easier turning into and out of London Road, the street in front came down to the basement, hence today's split levels. The occupants generally ran small shops, though one in the mid-19th century had kept a dame school. By 1890 the block was derelict and a year later it was demolished.

The original use of this island site, however, was for a forge, first recorded in 1475 when William Essex held it. Such isolation was essential in the days of timber construction and thatched rooves, for fear of fire. Being at the entrance to the then town was good for passing trade – horses that had shed a shoe, for example, or metalwork on vehicles needing running repairs. The cottages took its place when the forge moved across to the top of West Street. Constitutional Buildings is listed grade 2.

Constitutional Buildings in or soon after 1903, with Judges Terrace [38 and 39] in the background and what seems to be the shop staff posing with some of the stock outside W. & H. King, cycle-makers at 2 London Road on the right.

1-2 JUDGES TERRACE

This building, partly behind Constitutional Buildings, originated as a three-bay hall-house whose timbers have been tree-ring dated to the winter of 1447-8. It was extended five feet to the west very soon after being built. In the mid-16th century a first floor and chimney were inserted and in the mid-18th the present brick façade was added. Its position west of the former southern extension of London Road, now the access to a doctors' surgery, shows that it was an addition to the original layout of the borough.

The first documentary reference is in 1564, when it counted as one burgage, owned and occupied by William Stanford. He, or a namesake, is recorded in 1524 with goods worth £2, at the lower end of the scale of prosperity. The goods were probably stock in trade but we do not know his occupation, nor the early use of the building.

In the 17th century it was the residence of persons of some social standing, one of whom, Jeremy Johnson, recorded the date 1674 and his and his wife Alice's initials on the overmantel shortly after obtaining posssession. From ironworking at Woodcock Forge at Felbridge (now Wiremill) from 1664 to 1701 he made enough money to afford such a prestigious town house.

In the 19th century it was occupied by tradesmen, becoming a private house again early in the 20th century until converted to solicitors' offices in about 1960. It is now a private residence again, listed grade 2.

No early name is known for the building. The name Judges Terrace, from the tradition that the assize judges stayed here, has not been found before 1885.

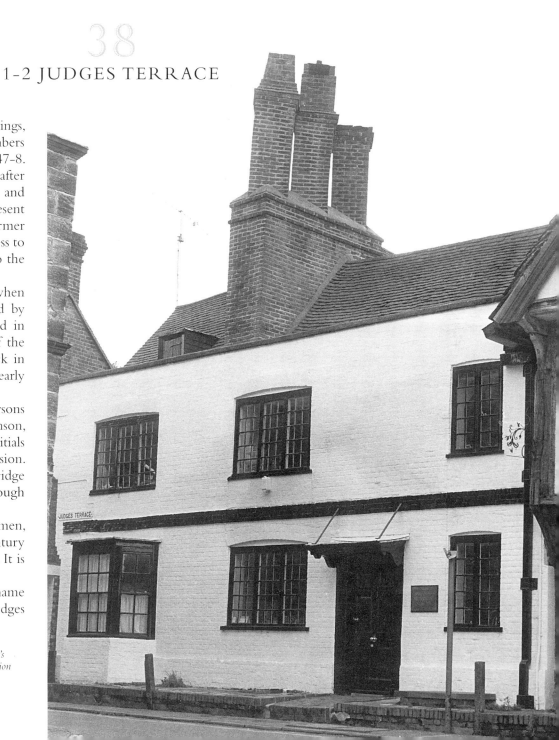

1-2 Judges Terrace in 1975, photographed for the East Grinstead Society's photographic record of every building in the original High Street conservation area.

CLARENDON HOUSE, 3 Judges Terrace

Clarendon House, the finest building of its date in the town, has been tree-ring dated to about 1455. It was built at the then fashionable end of the street as an open-hall house in the style known as Wealden, i.e. with floored bays at each end projecting forwards, something only a wealthy client could afford. That client was almost certainly the Fraternity of St Katherine, a religious and philanthropic organisation with its own altar and chaplain in the parish church. The fraternity, whose headquarters it would have been, definitely owned it in 1548 when all such bodies were dissolved and their property confiscated by the crown.

It was then an inn, the *George*, as it had probably been all along. Old inns of that name usually occupy prime sites and would have been the first seen when entering a town, as here before London Road was built up. Our *George* was speedily acquired by the Sackville family and continued for nearly another hundred years as East Grinstead's principal inn. In about 1561-6, the tree rings show, the hall was floored over.

After being acquired by Robert Pickering in 1630 it became a private house and was extended in stone soon after and the gables and projecting first-floor windows were added. By the end of the 18th century it was the home of William Pobgee, a currier, followed by people with a variety of occupations.

In an undated early photograph it is called De La Warr House but by 1885 it had its present name. Why Clarendon is not known.

In 1939 Clarendon House was thoroughly restored and the front was stripped to reveal the original timbering. A canteen for members of the armed forces and civil defence was created in it in 1940, transmuted after the war into a restaurant. In 1968 it was sold and became solicitor's offices, as it still is at the time of writing, listed grade 2.

Clarendon House as a restaurant in 1952, including the stone extension of 1630.

OLD STONE HOUSE, Judges Terrace

The original, eastern, part of Old Stone House was built as a crosswing to Clarendon House by Robert Pickering. Local sandstone was used rather than old-fashioned timber-framing for a building two bays deep with its rear façade as impressive as the frontage. The front rooms were panelled and heated, the fine staircase is still in use, and the Horsham stone roof survives.

Robert Pickering had acquired the property in 1630 by paying a shilling to the Earl of Dorset and £40 to Richard Amherst. Previously it had been part of the *George* but Pickering converted it to a high-status private residence. He is always styled 'Mr' or 'gent' in records and twice served as bailiff of the borough, the nearest thing East Grinstead had to a mayor.

In the early 1880s William Rudge, a prosperous local auctioneer, separated the building from Clarendon House and extended it sympathetically westwards. It is probably he who gave the name Old Stone House, first recorded in 1885.

He was succeeded by Dr Percy Evershed Wallis, who had his surgery in the front room of the original portion. He and his daughters, Miss Iris Wallis and Mrs Mabel Louisa Dempster, all took a leading part in public life. The Evershed Wallis ward at the Queen Victoria Hospital [9] is named in honour of his nephew, Dr W.E. Wallis.

After the first Dr Wallis, Old Stone House was acquired by Dr Spencer Lewis Walker, who had founded East Grinstead's first scout troop in 1908 and who became the movement's national physical training adviser, with a demonstration team of local members. He too was prominently involved in public service.

In the 1960s Clarendon House and Old Stone House were re-united to become the prestigious solicitor's offices they are today, listed grade 2 and unfortunately as attractive to pigeons as to humans.

Judges Terrace in the late 1920s, showing (left to right) nos 1–2, Clarendon House (with rendered front), the original portion of Old Stone House and the 19th-century extension.

Dr S.L. Walker (c.1881-1967) in his First World War uniform.

THE SHIP

The deeds of the *Ship* start as far back as 1642. No sign is named, but the occupant, Aptott Catt, is known to have been an alehouse-keeper in the previous year. As was usual at the time, he also had a trade, tailoring, as recorded in 1636 and 50.

In 1677 we first meet a name for the premises, the *Spread Eagle*, which by 1696 had changed to the *Ship*. This shows there is no foundation for the 20th-century theory that local pronunciation of an imagined original Sheep Lane as Ship Lane, as found in documents, accounts for the pub's name.

The present building dates from late Victorian times, with a row of porthole-type windows exemplifying the sense of fun that characterised what we think of as a solemn period of history.

Despite having such a long run of deeds and the names of most of the innkeepers, very little information has survived to bring the place to life, though the mid-19th-century censuses give some impression. In 1851 Samuel Winser, his wife and daughter ran the *Ship* with a niece as servant and a living-in ostler to attend to horses. A widowed wire-maker and an unmarried labourer were there on census night, probably long-term residents, together with four 'travellers' – a married couple aged 24 and 23 and two unmarried men aged 23 and 22 – probably travellers in the sense in which we use the word today. In 1861 Charles Wood, his wife, four sons and a servant were looking after 23 lodgers – 16 males and seven females, of whom two were children with their mothers. There were two unaccompanied married women of no stated occupation and one married couple. The rest were single men, mostly labourers or building workers. It must have been about this time that the Mother Superior of St Margaret's persuaded the landlord to improve the accommodation and stop putting unrelated men, women and children in the same rooms, with the prospect of refusing to send people there if he did not comply. Soon she was starting evening classes for the residents and sometimes reading aloud to them.

In 2001 the *Ship* was closed for a four-month refurbishment costing £½ million.

The Ship in 1907 with Zion Cottage (demolished 1934) photographed across the front of Judges Terrace.

ZION CHAPEL

The chapel c. 1880, before the vestibule was added and the railings removed, also showing the manse on the left and the hall on the right, photographed by M.A. Melville.

Zion Chapel, opposite the *Ship*, was built in 1810 by the Burt family of Forest Row, wealthy brewers and bankers, and is East Grinstead's oldest surviving Nonconformist place of worship. It is a good example of a then fashionable style, built in brick with a form of roof structure pioneered in the Midlands but at that date hardly seen in southern England. The architect is unknown but there is good reason to think it was the East Grinstead builder and surveyor James Sanderson in the light of buildings he designed at Forest Row (now lost) and Sheffield Place. The small hall alongside was built in 1862 and the vestibule in front in 1911.

Almost from the start Zion Chapel was in the Countess of Huntingdon's Connexion, a body of Calvinistic Methodists, until doctrinal disagreements in the 1970s meant the congregation had to leave the Connexion and the building. It was then acquired by the revitalised local Baptist community, which initiated restoration work still in progress at the time of writing.

For most of the 19th century Zion Chapel was an important focus for alternatives to East Grinstead's religious, political and social establishment. Its Sunday School, founded in 1811, seventy years before compulsory schooling, and the further education initiatives it supported, provided rare opportunities for self-improvement. The full participation of lay people in running its affairs and speaking in public trained tradesmen and others for service in local government and leading roles in other areas of community life.

Today the grade 2 listed chapel, from a period ill-represented among East Grinstead's buildings, is an important part of the town's heritage.

GROVE HOUSE, 80 West Street

Grove House, further down West Street and on the opposite side, stands 12 feet above the modern street and the cellar floor stands four feet above it. Brick and sandstone steps and wrought-iron railings lead up to the front door on the original road level.

The brick building we see from below is a forward extension of an earlier structure, with lath and plaster walls, probably timber-framed. On a rear wall is a stone plaque inscribed 'H. B 1837 SHIP FOLLEY'. This dates the extension and indicates who was responsible for it, Henry Barber, recorded as landlord of the *Ship* [41] from 1831 until his death in 1842, 'a victim of strong drink'. Why he thought of his house as a folly is a mystery.

The name had been changed by 1845, when it was the residence of the Rev. James Blomfield, minister of Zion Chapel [42] from 1841 to 44. He ran a private school there, Grove House Academy, a Nonconformist alternative to the existing Anglican schooling and probably operating beyond the elementary level. He left East Grinstead in 1848 and died at Herne Bay in 1859 aged 72.

By 1871 Grove House was the home and studio of Henry Thomas Melville, a professional photographer from Bromley, some of whose work is reproduced in modern books of old local photographs. In 1873 he moved to Moat Road, and when he died in 1878, aged 45, his widow Mary Ann Melville carried on the business for another four or five years. The photograph of Zion Chapel and Manse on the previous page is her work.

Grove House was listed grade 2 in 1972.

Grove House in June 2005, photographed for this book by S.R. Kerr.

THE QUEENS ROAD CEMETERY CHAPELS (THE BELFRY), off West Street

In 1868 East Grinstead's overcrowded churchyard was closed to further burials and a Burial Board was soon set up by the ratepayers to create an alternative. The site acquired, part of the Swan Mead, was brought into use in 1869, approached by a new road called Cemetery Road until in 1887 its residents took advantage of Queen Victoria's jubilee to rename it Queens Road. Today, however, the only entrance is at the far end of West Street, on the opposite side from Grove House.

As was customary, one part was consecrated, for Church of England burials, reserving the unconsecrated part for Nonconformists and all others. Similarly there were two chapels, designed by the architectural practice of Parsons of Lewes, which had already designed the town's schools, now the Chequer Mead Arts Centre [5]. In what might be called an enriched Early English style, they formed a well-proportioned ensemble standing either side of a through-passage under a steep bell-cote. This *porte-cochère* enabled hearses and carriages to deliver coffins and mourners in the dry. In 1879 a small lean-to mortuary was added on the south.

In 1916 the cemetery was closed, except for burials in private plots, and the chapels served as comparatively neglected council stores, which after local government reorganisation in 1974 faced demolition. In view of their architectural quality, structural soundness and visual worth, the East Grinstead Society determined to save them, applying for listing and looking for a potential beneficial use.

Listing was refused, for though good they were not outstanding, and interested takers, such as the boxing club, were unable to proceed. In the next decade, however, drainage and electricity were laid on and the chapels were converted to characterful private housing renamed the Belfry, conveniently sited near town centre amenities but away from traffic. The cemetery was fenced from sight either side of the drive to the chapels, though public access to the graves is possible as explained on a board at the gates.

The chapels from the north-east in the early 20th century, with the gravestone of Thomas Cramp [see 51] in the bottom left-hand corner, photographed by Arthur Harding and issued by him as a postcard.

THE RAILWAY VIADUCT

Immediately after the cemetery gates West Street becomes West Hill, from the bottom of which one has one's first sight of the Imberhorne, Copyhold or Hill Place viaduct. Garden Wood Road passes beneath, giving a chance to see its scale and quality at close quarters.

The viaduct was an essential part of the Lewes and East Grinstead Railway that opened in 1882, designed by John Wolfe-Barry and engineered by Joseph Firbank. Its 262-yard span consists of 10 arches built of bricks made from the clay in the field below. The crown of the highest arch is 93 feet above the tributary of the Medway that it crosses.

Work on the viaduct began in July 1879 and took at least a year. On 26 May 1880 Joseph Wickens of Ashurst Wood, aged about twenty, was wheeling a barrow of planks on top of the scaffolding when the legs of the barrow caught against a board and he fell about 45 feet with his load. Although some planks fractured his thigh they broke his fall and so saved his life. Exactly a month later an unnamed 16-year old, working underneath the viaduct, was struck in the loins by a shovel which fell from 40 or 50 feet above and 'supposedly injured his kidneys'. A scaffolding collapse was blamed for the death from dropsy two years later of one of the bricklayers, Jesse Gilbert.

When the line closed in 1958 the track over the viaduct was retained, for trains reversing from the low level station up the spur to the high level and for overnight and weekend parking of carriages used on locomotive-hauled commuter traffic between East Grinstead and London. This facility was no longer needed after electrification in 1987 and so, on 8 September 1992, British Railways, glad to be rid of an expensive liability listed grade 2 in 1989, handed the viaduct over to the Bluebell Railway Extension Company. In 2002 the company had it put in order in expectation of soon bringing this imposing feat of engineering back into use and reinstating the line all the way back to East Grinstead.

The viaduct in the late 1950s or early '60s, photographed by Norman Sherry.

At the western end of the row of cottages in front of the church-yard entrance, 39 High Street is the easternmost of the burgages on the northern side of the High Street. It is also the first High Street property whose owner can be named, Katherine Roos in 1400. By then the family had been prominent here for seventy years but nothing else is known about Katherine.

From 1564 we have a run of names but no evidence of their occupations or how they used the building. A hundred years later their being styled 'Mr' or 'gent' suggests the property was wholly residential. At the start of the 19th century, however, it was a bank. It continued to house a bank counter when taken over by drapers and

grocers. It remained a grocer's until the 1970s.

An archaeological survey in 1997 concluded it was a modified L-shaped continuous-jettied house from the early 17th century, altered and fronted in brick in the 18th century (when it was also given a porch) and altered again after 1939. In 1996-7 the whole building was carefully restored but by then all the fine internal features noted in 1939 had long gone.

No. 39 retained intact its portland, all the way back to Institute Walk, right to the end of the 19th century. In July 1882 a commercial livestock market was established in a paddock behind the *Crown*, next door on the west. By 1899 it had absorbed the neighbouring portion of 39's portland, the northern stretch had been incorporated into the gardens of houses in Cantelupe Road, and the southern part was much the same medley of yard and outbuildings as today. Clearance of the site of the new Town Museum [71] permitted archaeological investigation of part of the portland but found only fragments of medieval pottery and late 19th-century material from the *Crown*.

No. 39 is listed grade 2.

39 High Street decorated for the 1911 coronation with all the staff lined up outside (photograph by Arthur Harding, issued as a postcard by the East Grinstead Society).

CROWN HOUSE, 35-37 High Street

mid-17th century one of only four businesses in East Grinstead to issue their own tokens to compensate for a national shortage of small change. By 1715 it had a billiard room, by 1739 a bowling green, and in 1766 it was reckoned 'as good an inn as any in Sussex'.

Towards the end of that century the old timber-framed building was largely rebuilt in brick, and in the 1880s the current third storey was created. To this day traces of a 15th- or 16th-century structure survive in the newspaper's reception area. There was access to the rear by a passage through the building on the left in the photograph.

It was never a regular coaching inn but it was the market inn right up to 1970, with a purpose-built market room added in 1853. During the 19th century that room also served for the magistrates' court, public meetings and dinners, manorial courts and private balls. At one of the latter, in 1885, electric light was specially installed, the first time it had been seen in East Grinstead. Several friendly societies had their headquarters here too, but as the century wore on it came to specialise in catering for commercial travellers, hence the inscription over the entrance in the photograph.

Crown House, next to no.39 and currently shared by *Bar Kuba*, the *East Grinstead Courier* and various offices, was once the town's principal inn, the oldest known by name in East Grinstead's history, the *Crown*.

In 1502 Thomas Langgerich bequeathed it to his wife Alice, and members of his family continued to hold it for more than two hundred years after that, usually in partnership with someone else. Its importance is shown by its being in 1636 one of only two taverns in the town, superior establishments licensed to serve wine, and in the

As the relief road, opened in 1978, took through-traffic the residential business of the *Crown* declined and so it was converted from an hotel to offices and a small pub, still at first with the same name. It was listed grade 2 in 1979.

The Crown *photographed by William Harding c.1864 (as reproduced by his son Arthur as a postcard in the early 20th century).*

7-11 HIGH STREET

This building, on the same side of the street as the *Crown* but almost at the far end, has been tree-ring dated to approximately 1455, with the eastern portion converted to its present 'cross-wing' form about ten years later. It was a four-bay structure of the Wealden type, originally with a Horsham stone roof, of which only the eastern end now survives. In 1828 the road was lowered and the building adapted with the steps and floor-levels we see today. In the same century shop-fronts were added. Excavations at the rear in 2001-2 found the ground so much disturbed by use and re-use that no firm conclusions could be drawn.

We do not know its original purpose, nor its use when first recorded in a document, the will of John Payne in 1558. By the 1640s William Croxton, a blacksmith, occupied it, though his forge was not necessarily here. After Robert Payne sold it in 1669 it passed through several hands until in 1748 Mary Driver sold it to Sackville Bale, acting to secure for the Duke of Dorset the voting right it carried. Successive occupants during that period included a shoemaker, a baker and a tailor.

By then it was two dwellings. Eighteenth-century records are few but in the 19th century the western part was occupied at different times by tailors, an ironmonger, a watchmaker and a draper and the eastern by a well-digger and rat-catcher, tailors, a currier, a plumber and a milliner. The 20th century saw the International grocer's until 1938, succeeded by an outfitter's, at the west end, and a tailor's followed by a hardware store that became a confectioner's at the other.

The building, which occupies one of the original burgage plots, is grade 2 listed.

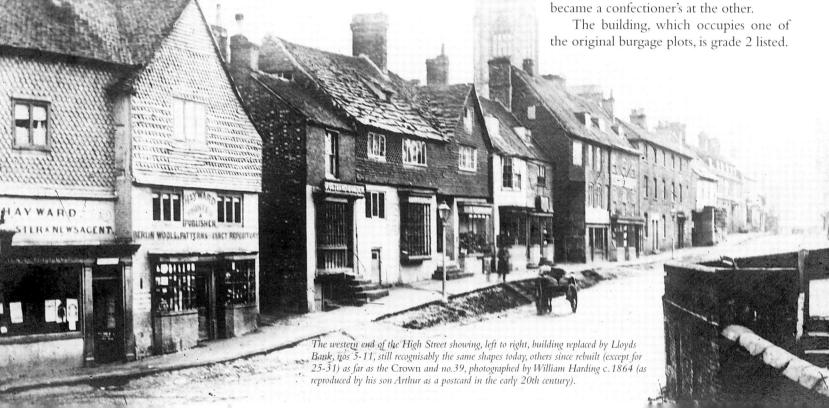

The western end of the High Street showing, left to right, building replaced by Lloyds Bank, nos 5-11, still recognisably the same shapes today, others since rebuilt (except for 25-31) as far as the Crown and no.39, photographed by William Harding c.1864 (as reproduced by his son Arthur as a postcard in the early 20th century).

THE WHITEHALL, 45-53 London Road

Round the corner from the High Street, in the different world of London Road, the Whitehall, with its stylish façade, was the centre of the darkest day in East Grinstead's history. Shortly after 5 p.m. on 9 July a German plane dropped 10 bombs across the town, two of which fell in the auditorium of the cinema at the back of the building. 108 lives were lost and 235 people were injured. About one third of the victims were service personnel, one third adult civilians and one third children. The cinema was destroyed, the façade escaped virtually unscathed, and the rooms between were damaged.

The cinema originated as a theatre, opened in 1910 and was at first also used for roller-skating. It was part of a redevelopment by Messrs Letheby & Christopher, the racecourse caterers, of the Grosvenor Hall and restaurant which had been built in 1883. As films became more popular, however, the floor was sloped and 'the pictures' became its main business instead of a subsidiary part of it.

In 1936 adjoining properties were acquired and the Whitehall Parade was created by the eminent cinema architect M.F. Edwardes Jones, a sequence of shops with flats above. A large restaurant, function rooms and the Rainbow Ballroom were also part of the new complex, with the theatre unchanged.

Many leading entertainers performed there over the years. The composer Hamilton Harty was the accompanist at the concert on the opening night and Vera Lynn took part in the final live performance in 1940.

The cinema was never rebuilt, and over the next half-century the restaurant and ballroom gave way to more shops, offices and a nightclub. In 1993 the East Grinstead Society marked the 50th anniversary of the bombing with a plaque by the main entrance and a short unveiling ceremony.

Whitehall Parade when new in 1937.

93-101 LONDON ROAD

Passers-by probably give little attention to this block of shops with flats over, certainly not above the ground floor. It is a fairly typical shopping parade of its period, erected in 1935 as part of the development of the Christopher estate by Messrs Letheby & Christopher, the proprietors of the Whitehall [49] further up London Road. The main developments were in Christopher Road and King Street: housing, Caffyns' garage and the Radio Centre cinema that preceded today's Atrium, all influenced by the fashionable Art Deco style of the time.

The proportions and brickwork of 93-101 London Road are good examples too, with the blue glazed ceramic tiles on the roof particularly characteristic, though now in not exactly pristine condition. Less expensive slate tiles are used at the back, but the blue ones on the front were too much for local people and consistently execrated throughout the remainder of the 1930s, through the '40s and well on into the '50s. In the war it was even claimed by some that their glazed surface would reflect the moonlight during the blackout and so identify the town as a target!

Gradually they were ignored and forgotten but perhaps today we should hail this block as one of the town's best representatives of its period and hope to see it better appreciated. Having lost the cinema in 1989, we are not over-endowed with thirties buildings of quality.

London Road c. 1936-7, showing, on the right, nos 93-101, the tall building between the Co-op put up in 1931 (background) and Duncans in a building from 1925.

THE CLOCKTOWER, London Road

The clocktower in January 1974, with the original railway bridge on the left and the gasworks water-tower (demolished in 1978) in the background.

Thomas Cramp

Further along London Road, by the footbridge over the relief road, stands a small and not very inspired brick tower bearing a clock subscribed for in 1890 to honour the 80th birthday of Thomas Cramp.

Thomas was born in Lewes and apprenticed in 1825 to Richard Palmer, a stationer in Brighton. Before the year's end his master was dead, so Richard's brother William, in the same business in East Grinstead High Street [12], took him on.

From 1832 Thomas Cramp taught in the Sunday School of Zion Chapel [42], influencing generations of youths who became prominent townsmen. In 1837 he took up teetotalism, soon founding the East Grinstead Total Abstinence Society. This comparatively new practice was incomprehensible to most people. Members were stoned in the streets and Cramp was suspended from the chapel, though he lived to see his cause widely accepted. By thrift and hard work he prospered, involved in most local institutions and good causes. He held office in the savings bank, gas company, dispensary, Public Hall Company and Burial and School Boards. He also served the local branch of the Bible Society, successive literary and scientific institutions and the divisional Liberal Association, in addition to building many inexpensive houses for rent in West Street and Railway Approach.

Cramp's public spirit and adherence to principle won the respect of people of all persuasions, so that in 1887 his temperance jubilee was publicly celebrated. In 1891 he died, having seen the clock erected on the Institute, on the corner between London Road and the site of Caffyns' garage.

When the Institute was demolished in 1938 the clock was stored for want of any alternative location. In 1955 Mr Sidney Betchley and Mr L.W.E. Dungey solved the problem by funding the tower from which it still hangs, including a slightly inaccurate explanatory plaque.

The clock proved increasingly unreliable, until in 2000 it was completely restored thanks to an anonymous benefactor in co-operation with the Town Council, with a second plaque tacitly correcting the earlier one.

MCDONALD'S, 163-67 London Road

Over the footbridge and further along London Road one comes to McDonald's. In the year 2000 that company paid £1.95 million to buy and convert the premises, despite vigorous opposition, ostensibly on traffic, litter and environmental grounds.

Previously it had been the *White Lion* public house, erected in 1965 by the local branch of Y.J. Lovell Ltd to a standard design for Watneys the brewers. An identical building is to be found at Rottingdean. In keeping with the then latest trends it served food. For a time in 1988 the landlord kept sheep in the garden, which also had a pond, probably originating from digging for brickearth, which was once common in this part of East Grinstead.

In 1953 Watneys had acquired the older pub of the same name which stood flush against the road on the same site. That, in turn, was a late 19th-century rebuilding for the Southdown and East Grinstead Breweries of a twice-extended earlier *White Lion*, which, judging by the photograph here, was first put up in the 18th century.

The deeds of the property date from 1710 but the name is not recorded until 1730, when it was appointed to be the meeting place of the trustees of the turnpike road running past it, to us the A22. It was a good spot for an inn, at the point where East Grinstead Common met the edge of the town, a welcome sight for hungry, thirsty or weary travellers. By 1875, when the built-up area had engulfed it, it had become the headquarters of the local Bonfire Boys, who paraded from it to the Playfield every 5 November with bands, banners, torches, fancy dress and blazing tar-barrels.

The White Lion *in the 1860s, photographed by William Harding.*

MOAT CHURCH

Moat Church, next but one to McDonald's, was built by Edward Steer, who in about 1862 bought part of Moat Farm, laid out the first stretch of Moat Road here and began erecting 'villa residences' along it.

Steer, a teetotaller and Nonconformist ally of Thomas Cramp, anxious that their value should not be adversely affected by the building of a public house on this corner, sold the plot to Congregationalists looking for a site for a church in East Grinstead. In April 1870 the building was ready, designed and built by Steer in a mild gothic style and with his family and four of his workmen and their wives forming half the regular attenders. Because it was built on a damp hollow, probably the result of digging for brickearth, the church has a liberal supply of buttresses and had an extra large one added in 1914. A Sunday School hall was provided alongside in 1874, and vestries and other rooms were built facing Moat Road in a pleasant Edwardian manner in 1905.

Beyond them a manse for the minister was built in 1878 but in 1927 it was sold and currently houses a dentist's surgery. The stone spire was covered in shingles in 1961.

By 1923 complaints of passing traffic noise and vibration began but the congregation has consistently turned down proposals to move.

During the ensuing three decades Moat Church nourished three young men who were to gain distinction in the ministry: John Marsh, a theologian who became Principal of Mansfield College, Oxford, Erik Routley, a hymnologist who was president of the Congregational Church in England and Wales 1970-1, and Bernard Thorogood, a missionary who in 1979-80 served as moderator of the United Reformed Church created by the merger of the Congregational Union and the Presbyterian Church of England.

Moat Church in the 1920s.

TRINITY METHODIST CHURCH,
London Road/Lingfield Road

Further along London Road, on the corner with Lingfield Road, Trinity Methodist Church saw considerable re-building in 2004-5 to provide space for expansion of its work and witness, in style and materials sympathetic to the core worship area.

East Grinstead's first Methodist church opened in 1881, in London Road where W.H. Smith's currently stands, but in 1929 the question arose of a new, easier to maintain, building in a quieter location. In 1936 the trustees purchased Southwick House and its grounds, subsequently giving the county council a corner of the site to improve the junction and selling the house (since replaced by flats) to the Urban District Council for civil defence requirements.

The main structure was built of local stock brick with hand-made sand-faced roof tiles by the local builders F.W. Honour & Son, both of whom were trustees, to a design by H.R. Houchin. Side-aisles and a shallow chancel and transepts follow traditional ground-plans but the clean uncluttered lines in vogue at the time make it well suited to Methodist principles of worship. A polygonal vaulted ceiling and a sloping wood-block floor are other contemporary features. The brick columns were the work of another trustee, Arthur Clarke, a bricklayer by trade.

With permanent seating for 130 and space for 40 chairs, it was opened on 31 August 1938. Vestries, classrooms, kitchens and offices linked the church to a hall on the Lingfield Road side. During the war this hall served as the civil defence canteen. In 1970 it was renamed the Lingfield Hall and additional buildings on the other side were named the Crawley Down Hall as the chapels in those villages closed. In 1977 there was further enlargement. Growing attendances had made two morning services necessary in 1969 and required another extension in 1980 to accommodate another 50 worshippers.

A manse for the minister was provided alongside in the 1960s and a centenary history by W.H. Irvine was published in 1981.

Trinity Methodist Church seen through the open main doors in July 1975.

LINGFIELD ROAD POST OFFICE STORES

A little way down Lingfield Road, on the corner of Durkins Road, stands a shop which was a sub-post office for almost 120 years.

The building was in existence by 1886, named Wellington House in recognition of its location in the area known since at least 1776 as Wellington Town. It was built for James Morris, a grocer and tailor, who had previously had a shop a little further south. In its grounds stood a fine tree, a highly appropriate Wellingtonia. In January 1887, as the building-up of Lingfield Road and its surroundings intensified, Morris met an increasing need by taking on the duties of postmaster.

On his death in 1906, while serving his third year as an Urban District councillor, his daughter Joanna took on the postal side and his son Victor Emmanuel the grocer's. Victor's christian names were those of the first king of united Italy, a hero of English Liberals such as James Morris and his son. Victor was also a Nonconformist and a pacifist. When called up in 1916 he refused to be conscripted on religious grounds and was set on government work. He was also a prize-winning amateur photographer and picture-postcard publisher, some of whose work has been republished in the modern books of old local photographs.

In the Second World War Victor Morris sold the business to the local mini-chain of high-class grocers Taylor and Bristow, who attracted customers from across the town. When Mr Peter Bristow retired in 1979 the shop became a Spar convenience store that has outlived almost all the other small shops in this quarter of the town. Despite losing the post office counter in 2004 it flourishes in the hands of the second generation of the Patel family.

The shop in the early 20th century, photographed by Victor Morris and issued by him as a postcard.

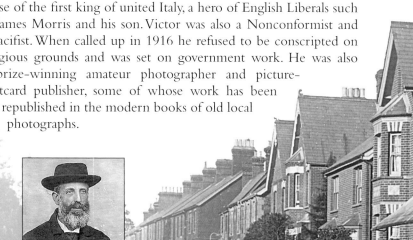

*James Morris
(1838-1906)*

IMBERHORNE LOWER SCHOOL, Windmill Lane

Across the recreation ground from the Lingfield Road stores stands the former County Grammar School, now housing the first three years of Imberhorne School. It was designed by East Sussex County Council's architect's department and opened in 1928 to serve

Richard L. Treble (1879-1941), the school's first headmaster, on his retirement in July 1938, photographed by Harold Connold.

The Grammar School in the early 1950s, photographed by Jonathan Hames of Feltham.

to be viable it had to be mixed, when single-sex secondary schools were the norm, but with girls and boys taught in separate classrooms in separate quadrangles with a hedge down the middle of the field. There were even separate common rooms for the masters and mistresses.

By the Second World War some of these distinctions had gone and pupils were gaining entry to universities and other higher education and entering the professions. Under the 1944 Education Act fees were abolished and selection was on merit alone as measured by the Eleven Plus examination and interview. A technical section for boys from secondary modern schools tested at 13 was created in huts in the grounds.

As the movement for comprehensive schools proved irresistible in the 1960s there was some thought of making the premises a sixth form college but numbers likely to stay on made that impracticable. Instead, as from September 1970, this building took all 11-year-olds from the western part of the town and the villages to its south and west, from where they went on, aged 13, to the former secondary modern buildings

children aged 11 and over who had passed an entrance examination or whose parents were able and willing to pay fees. Its style was that favoured for such establishments for some three decades, grander and more spacious than those in which their contemporaries would stay until the leaving age, fourteen.

Because north-eastern Sussex was comparatively thinly populated, it served everywhere within an arc from Groombridge in the east to Nutley in the south and Three Bridges in the west. Even so,

in Imberhorne Lane. This created one comprehensive school, Imberhorne, on two sites. At the same time Sackville secondary modern in Lewes Road took all the 11-year-olds from the rest of the town and the villages to its south and south-east to form a matching comprehensive.

Although no timetable has been set, it seems certain that Imberhorne Lower School will be housed in new buildings on the main site and the Windmill Lane premises sold for housing.

BALDWINS HILL SCHOOL, Lowdells Lane

With its grounds backing on to those of Imberhorne Lower School, the original and present premises of Baldwins Hill School are reached by walking the unmade stretch of Windmill Lane.

Until 1993 Baldwins Hill lay half in East Grinstead and Sussex and half in Lingfield and Surrey. As settlement in the area grew, the Lowdell family charity founded a school in Windmill Lane in January 1874 for children from both sides of the border within a quarter-mile radius. It was run as a Church of England School with 36 pupils – 20 girls and 16 boys – and one teacher, Miss Elizabeth Matilda Moultrie. Two older pupils assisted her as monitors, paid a shilling a week.

The building soon proved inadequate and was taken over by the Lingfield School Board,

Baldwins Hill School from the north-west in June 2005, photographed for this book by S.R. Kerr.

which had been founded in 1880 to provide elementary education funded from the rates. The present core buildings in Lowdells Lane were opened in April 1898. The original premises then became an institute, a sort of community centre for the area. They are now a private residence, Bell House, so called from the little turret that housed the school bell.

In due course Surrey County Council took over from the school boards and Baldwins Hill School became a primary school, as it is today. When the whole area became part of West Sussex in 1993 the school was extended and improved, the playing field on the other side of Lowdells Lane was sold for housing, and part of the adjoining Imberhorne Lower School fields was made available in replacement. This involved grubbing up the hedge that had formed the county boundary for perhaps a thousand years.

In September 2004 Baldwins Hill School and Halsford Park School in the town pioneered locally the new concept of 'federated leadership', sharing a common head and deputy head but otherwise still separate.

ST MARY'S CHURCH, Windmill Lane

St Mary's church, in the made-up part of Windmill Lane, was designed by the architect William Thorold Lowdell, a member of the local family that provided the original Baldwins Hill School and gave name to the road past its present premises.

The Stenning family, whose prosperous timber business enabled them to take a leading part in local life, seeing a need for an Anglican church in the growing area of East Grinstead in which they lived, provided the site and much of the initial finance. The foundation stone was laid in 1891 and construction, of brick with local sandstone features and in a 13th-century style, began from the east end, adding bays westwards as funds permitted. A hut used by the navvy mission during the building of our railway to Oxted in the early 1880s was moved from the adjoining recreation ground to act as a temporary nave. In 1905 the church was consecrated and a parish was formed. Seven years later the building was completed, apart from the addition of a choir vestry in 1928, and the hut had been re-erected beside the church to serve as its hall.

Several internal features were designed by eminent artists. Some of the stained glass is by Geoffrey Webb, whose home and studio were in East Grinstead [24], the high altar was the work of G.H. Fellowes-Prynne in 1918, and Sir Ninian Comper created a side altar and rich baldacchino in 1952. All the fittings reflect St Mary's high church tradition and the workmanship throughout is of a high standard. The building, which is not listed, is normally open during daylight hours.

The Rev. R.R. Needham photographed by R.J. McKenzie in 1938.

Perhaps the most noteworthy vicar of St Mary's was the Rev. Robert Raikes Needham, there from 1927 to 1929, who, although he then retired through ill-health, aged 70, lived to complete his century. In 1938 he published his autobiography *Just for Remembrance*, in which he devotes five pages to his time here and prints photographs of the high altar and the memorial to his parents.

St Mary's church, not quite completed, hall and vicarage seen from Lingfield Road recreation ground c. 1905-10.

ST MARY'S SCHOOL, Windmill Lane

The core of St Mary's Church of England Primary School is the stylish hall designed for the adjoining church by Arnold Mitchell in 1923.

St Mary's began its life as North End School, founded in 1885 by Mrs Stenning to provide elementary education on Anglican principles. That building still stands, between nos 6 and 7 North End, with its original name on a plaque over the entrance. Following a spell as the adult education centre, it currently houses Fledglings day nursery and pre-school.

After the Second World War the growing population in that part of East Grinstead and higher standards and expectations for primary schools showed up the inadequacies of the two-classroom building and its restricted site. It was therefore decided to re-locate to the extensive grounds of St Mary's church, building onto and behind the hall, with a playground at the rear and a games field behind that. The parish, the diocese of Chichester and East Sussex County Council all bore a share of the costs of the building while the county alone funded the play areas and kitchen.

Building began in the summer of 1954 and the school came into use in the following February. It comprised a canteen, staff common room and three classrooms, with a fourth planned so as to accommodate up to 120 children. The architect was Hilton Wright and the builders F.W. Honour & Sons Ltd of East Grinstead. The estimated cost was about £13,000. On 25 February 1956 there was an official ceremony including blessing of the classrooms by the Bishop of Chichester and a speech by East Grinstead's M.P., the Hon. Mrs Evelyn Emmett, who spoke of the atomic age that the pupils would inherit. One of them, Jennifer Lulham, gave her a bouquet.

A replacement hall was built where the hut stood. The school, which retains close links with the church, has since been enlarged and modernised and is sought after by parents within a wide radius.

St Mary's church hall, as adapted and extended to be the heart of the school, in June 2005, photographed for this book by S.R. Kerr.

THE OLD PEST HOUSE, 52 Dorset Avenue

In Dorset Avenue, further down London Road and parallel to Windmill Lane, one comes unexpectedly among 1930s housing upon a charming late 18th-century building, now a characterful private house. When first built, however, financed from the rates, it stood solitary in the middle of the Common, for it was the pest house for the parish of East Grinstead, the earliest form of isolation hospital. People with infectious diseases had to live in it, looking after themselves, until they were cured – or dead. A nearby spring probably helped in selecting its site, for otherwise a well would have had to be dug.

In the 1821 census the Pest House was occupied by three agricultural families totalling seven males and ten females, presumably 'cases'. Its sale was authorised in 1861, by which time inoculation was commonplace, sanitation was generally being improved and medical care was becoming more sophisticated.

The Pest House in the second half of the 20th century, photographed by P.D. Wood.

The Old Pest House is exceptionally well constructed of local hand-made bricks with tile-hanging at first-floor level as in most vernacular buildings in this part of the Weald. It is now deservedly listed grade 2.

THE SPACE HOUSE, Pine Grove

The Space House in 1973, photographed by C.W. Goolden.

(1886-1969). It has been described as a classic modern building and 'iconic', a rare distinction for a privately owned dwelling, and was the prototype for three houses built about a year later near Windsor.

A steel frame clasps the whole house, holding it off the ground. It has an H-shaped plan, all on one level and with a flat roof. The walls, floors and roof are timber-framed, with Western Red Cedar Boarding and quarter-inch polished plate-glass windows creating a light, spacious and tranquil atmosphere. The structure has lent itself to re-configuring the layout without doing violence to the original design. Including four bedrooms and two bathrooms, it was sold at auction early in 1965 for £6,500 and again in 1968 for £12,750. The current owners, who bought it in 2002, are only the fourth in its history.

I do not know the reasons for the choice of name, but extra-terrestrial space was one of the great new preoccupations of the 1960s and spaciousness is one of the house's characteristics.

In September 2002 the Space House was the Twentieth Century Society's building of the month and in June 2003 it was one of the highlights of National Architectural Week. No doubt in time to come it will be considered worthy of listing.

A good way further down London Road, at the far end of Pine Grove, is the Space House, probably the most futuristic building in East Grinstead. It was designed in 1963-4 by the architects Peter Foggo and David Thomas, who had graduated from Liverpool in 1959 and were inspired by the work of Ludwig Mies van der Rohe

FELBRIDGE BRIDGE

Turning left at the end of Pine Grove one regains London Road and immediately after the hotel comes upon the bridge. 'Where is the bridge at Felbridge?' people sometimes ask, so accustomed to travelling by car they never notice as the A22 takes them across it where Surrey meets Sussex. The pedestrian cannot fail to see it, perhaps with disappointment at its lack of grandeur.

Felbridge is the fourth oldest bridge-name recorded in Sussex, *c.*1135-54, a good six centuries before anything resembling the village named after it. Its antiquity implies an important road, which the main road from London to the nearest points on the south coast always has been. Its name means the bridge by the Feld, the open land. That area, which also gave name to the Felesmere of Domesday Book and to Felcourt, included what became East Grinstead Common, stretching right up to the edge of the town.

No early name is known for the river which runs under the bridge, passes Lingfield and eventually joins the Medway. From at least the mid-18th century it was known for many years as Felbridge Water. The terms 'Fel River' or 'Fel Stream' have not been traced earlier than 1967 and should be avoided because they reverse the historical naming process.

The first depiction of the bridge on an accurately surveyed large-scale map is in Ogilby's *Britannia*, a book of road maps published in 1679. On Budgen's equally accurately surveyed map of Sussex in 1724, however, a ford is shown. Between those dates the bridge must have been damaged or destroyed, probably one of those swept away in the torrential rainfall that hit this part of the country throughout the day and night of 28 July 1703.

It was not until 1750 that Surrey and Sussex combined to rebuild the bridge. Investigation by the Felbridge and District History Group has shown that the present structure accords with a mid-18th century date, with widening in 1909 and the early 1970s. A plaque records the two counties' responsibility for its upkeep.

Felbridge bridge in the 1920s, the Star *in the background opposite its sign.*

NORTH END WORKING MEN'S CLUB,
32-33 North End

In 1861 Edmund Wise, a 46-year-old cottager born in Bath, was living somewhere in the area of East Grinstead Common that later developed as North End. The next year he opened the Sussex Brewery, producing ale and porter, at or near his home. By the 1871 census a gardener was living at the Brewery, while Wise's home was in Glen Vue Road, now known as Railway Approach, with George Coomber, a 29-year-old brewer born in East Grinsted, almost certainly Wise's manager, a few doors away. Ten years later, with development underway at North End, Coomber had moved into the re-titled, and possibly rebuilt, East Grinstead Brewery, which he continued to advertise until 1895.

In 1888, because breweries were not allowed to permit drinking on the premises or purchasing less than two gallons of beer at a time, he applied for an off-licence, arguing it was better to buy from him for home consumption than to go to the *Star* at Felbridge and stay there, but local temperance activists successfully opposed him. Mr Stenning, the timber-merchant who owned most of the land at North End, therefore suggested and facilitated forming a club, which was effected in July 1892 with 39 members, all apparently working men living nearby. At the same time Bushell & Co. of Westerham took over the brewery. By 1901 William G. West, a brewer's agent, was in the residential quarters and Coomber was at 21 North End, now dealing in milk!

At the fiftieth anniversary, in 1942, two of the original members, T. Coomber and C. Baldwin, were still in membership.

The derelict former brewery and club in June 2005, photographed for this book by S.R. Kerr.

A fire in 1987 wrecked the interior, days after it had been renovated, after which the building remained unoccupied. Thirteen years later the trustees were traced, with some difficulty, and the sale of the club, now the property of a registered friendly society, was agreed. The forlorn old building is unlikely to survive much longer.

LINGFIELD LODGE, London Road

Lingfield Lodge, opposite Trinity Methodist Church [54], seems to have been only recently built when the 1841 census was taken, presumably for the Rev. Robert Fitzherbert Fuller, Perpetual Curate of Lingfield, who was living there, aged 46, with his wife, three children and two servants. Ten years later his widow, Maria Ursula Fuller, was the head of household, remaining until at least 1858.

She was succeeded briefly by Superintendent William Kennard, who had been the town's sole policeman in the mid-1840s, and then from 1862 to his death in 1885 John Whyte, who had retired there from his medical practice at Wilmington House [29] in the High Street. After his widow died in 1904 it seems to have been empty for a time but by 1909 the Rev. Elijah Harrison Littlewood, who had retired as vicar of Biggleswade in 1903, was in residence. By the end of the First World War his widow was the householder, succeeded by their daughters in the 1920s. By 1934 Sir Eyre Hutson, K.C.M.G., a former governor of Fiji, was there, until his death in 1936, but by the time his widow died in 1951, not long after moving out, the house was derelict.

It was bought by the newly founded East Grinstead Housing Society Ltd for conversion to a retirement home at a time when such developments, as opposed to privately owned homes run for profit, were still quite new. On 13 June it was officially opened by the Rt Hon. Harold Macmillan who, as Housing Minister, was charged with solving a serious national shortage. In 1958 a new wing was built and in 1997 the conservatory at the front gained a new roof and windows.

Main front of Lingfield Lodge in June 2005, photographed for this book by S.R. Kerr.

OUR LADY AND ST PETER'S ROMAN CATHOLIC CHURCH,
London Road

The church of Our Lady and St Peter is the work of F.A. Walters, the architect of other Roman Catholic churches in Sussex, including earlier ones at Petworth and Brighton and later at Eastbourne and Herons Ghyll. Here, however, he deserted the gothic architecture he normally favoured for a simplified Romanesque effect, the only building in East Grinstead in that style. Perhaps this was to make a bold contrast with Moat Church [53] diagonally opposite, perhaps insisted on by his patron, Lady Blount.

Sir Edward and Lady Blount had bought Imberhorne Manor in 1878 and created in it a chapel dedicated to SS Edward the Confessor and Louis of France, royal saints of the countries where his banking business financed the early development of railways. In 1879 they opened it for public use so that their fellow Roman Catholics no longer had to travel to Crawley.

A church more accessibly located, and worthy of a growing congregation, was soon needed. Lady Blount died shortly after the laying of the foundation stone on 15 June 1897 but the building was opened in October 1898 and consecrated by the Bishop of Southwark in August 1899. The name must reflect Cardinal Vaughan's dedication of England to Our Lady and St Peter in 1893, with consequent demotion of St George. In practice, however, it is usually referred to simply as St Peter's, like the associated primary school which Sir Edward founded soon after opening the chapel.

Internally the church, which was redecorated for the centenary, is now uncluttered, light and dignified, as anyone can see, since it is normally open during the day. There was indignation when the outside was painted a shade of pink but, as predicted, the colour has naturally toned down since.

An attempt by the East Grinstead Society to have it listed was not successful.

The church in 1911, with in the foreground the garden fence of the Hollies, a house replaced by a parade of shops in 1928.

A few doors along from the Roman Catholic church, 174 London Road was built in 1894 for Richard Pennifold, a baker previously at 195 London Road, taking advantage of a corner space left when St James's Road was developed not long before.

It exemplifies the high standard of the ordinary building work of the period. The street faces are symmetrical and the proportions are aptly adjusted to the site. Materials and workmanship are excellent, with moulded bricks in the string-course and below the window sills, coved eaves and handsome chimney stacks. The dormer windows are disproportionately large, perhaps because that is where Richard's reclusive son Fred lived. The bakehouse and store were alongside St James's Road.

Their photographs show a not inappropriate intensity of gaze in both father and son, for Fred was a practising astrologer and his sister Rosa a phrenologist. Many local people had their horoscopes cast by the one and the bumps on their head interpreted by the other. At the same time both were involved with working with young people at Moat Church [53] across the road, encouraging them to make music and inspiring a lasting incentive to read great literature in the boy who was to become the Rev. Dr John Marsh. Their widower father was equally active in Nonconformist circles in the town.

In the mid-1920s the shop changed hands, remaining a baker's for half a century or so and still, in the late 1940s, when the splendidly named Charles Penberthy Towler ran it, willing to serve regular customers who knocked on the back door after closing. But there were no more 'faintly enigmatic personalities who seemed to breathe another air', as the Pennifolds were characterised by the late Raymond Wood.

174 London Road with the Roman Catholic church [65] in the background early in the 20th century. Inset: Richard Pennifold and, with his mandolin, his son Fred.

THE OLD STATION HOUSE, London Road

The Old Station House as a private dwelling in the 1960s or '70s.

It is not easy today to envisage this building, across the bridge over the relief road, as it originally was, the terminus of East Grinstead's first railway, opened from Three Bridges in 1855 by private enterprise. It was designed by R. Jacomb-Hood, the London, Brighton & South Coast Railway's engineer, uncharacteristically using local sandstone. The track came in along what is now the Worth Way and ended at a single platform with a very small verandah alongside the building.

The line was extended to Tunbridge Wells in 1866, through the cutting that now holds the Beeching Way relief road, and a new station was constructed with its entrance on the bridge above the tracks beside London Road. The original terminus became staff housing and the rails beside it became sidings. The wooden goods shed was replaced by a larger brick one. The new station closed in 1884 and was demolished, replaced by a two-level station on the site of the building we use today.

Closure of the Three Bridges-Tunbridge Wells line in 1967 made possible the relief road to divert through-traffic from the town centre. Construction of a slip road from London Road necessitated demolishing the goods shed, which the East Grinstead Society had been campaigning to preserve as a youth arts and drama centre. The original building became a private house until in 1982 it was very sympathetically extended at the rear for conversion to offices. In 2004 it became a clinic for slimming and other adjustments to people's bodies.

The whole scene symbolises the changing relations of road and rail over 150 years, from the railway's first impact in promoting the development of this part of the town to the still unresolved traffic problems of East Grinstead as a whole.

THE BROADWAY, London Road

The *Broadway*, as it is now called, next to the Old Station House, was built in 1939 by the brewers Ind Coope, who named it, in what is probably a unique tribute, the *Glanfield* after their architect, a resident of Dormans Park who in the previous year had rebuilt for them the *Rose and Crown* [13] in the High Street. The same sandstone features and skilful use of narrow bricks are found in both, employed at the *Broadway* to set off the Scottish Baronial stylistic influences apparent in the excellent slated roof and turret. At first the sign bore no illustration but in the late 1970s architect's equipment made it more eye-catching and informative.

Why in the next decade the wish for a new 'image' produced the name the *Broadway* does not seem to have been explained. The accompanying bold colour-scheme may be thought to obscure the building's architectural merits, but providing the previously empty forecourt with tables and seats has proved good for business and contributed to making this part of the town much more lively.

That forecourt is the site of the *Railway Hotel*, built in 1856 by the Croydon brewers Nalder and Collyer to exploit the potential of the town's first railway station [67] opened alongside in the previous year. By 1892 the *Railway Hotel* was advertising private apartments, hot, cold and shower baths, billiards, a tennis lawn, facilities for boarding and feeding horses, and carriages for hire. By 1909 a motor garage, a telephone and a croquet and bowling green had been added. AA recognition had been achieved by 1927 and a porter would meet

The Railway Hotel in or soon after 1903.

trains, but the station had moved to its present site more than forty years previously and demand for the *Railway*'s hotel facilities was in decline, hence its replacement by new proprietors.

To the casual passer-by, any interest in 104-108 London Road, just a little way past Railway Approach after the *Broadway*, must be what can be bought within. From across the road, however, several features catch the eye, notably the attractive gable in 17th-century Dutch style in the centre and the boarded-up corner turret on the right-hand building. Closer inspection reveals dates on rainwaterheads – 1903 in the centre and 1906 on the left.

The right-hand building, no.108, is the oldest, East Grinstead's first purpose-built fire station, erected early in the 20th century with funds collected by Arthur Hastie, a local solicitor who was the fire brigade secretary and owned the site. The turret housed an open-fronted lookout area facing up the road and across it to Hastie's house, Placelands. There was also a bell-cote on the ridge of the roof, now gone. By 1903, however, the fire station had relocated to 140 London Road (now replaced by an office block) and this building housed the London Central Meat Company. It was still a butcher's in the 1960s.

Nos 104-106 were also built for Hastie on his land, designed by the local architects Douglass and Mathews. Until the mid-1920s the gabled one was the Excelsior Boot Stores, owned by Walter John Wilson Hitch. For about a decade it continued as a shoe-shop. Through the second half of the century it was a ladies' hairdresser's.

The left-hand one was in business by 1905, as the refreshment rooms of the baker William Curtis, who also had shops in De La Warr Road and West Street. It has now achieved its century in the same use. The room above the shop served at times as a religious meeting place: the Free Church Girls' Guild before the First World War, then what became the Gospel Protestant Mission, and later, in the 1950s, the home of another independent cause.

There is more to some of East Grinstead's shops than most people suspect!

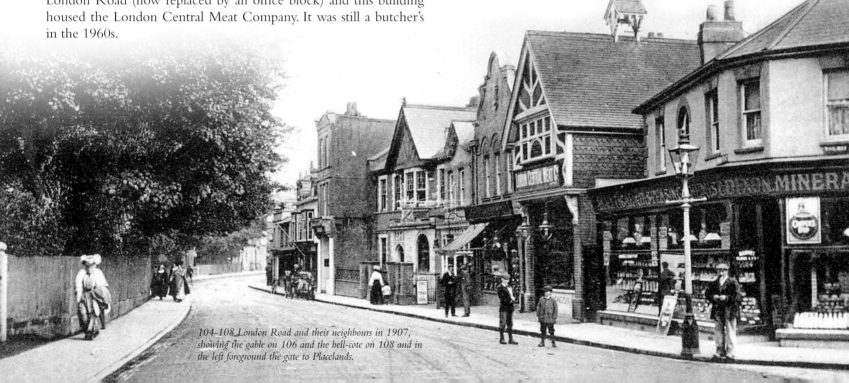

104-108 London Road and their neighbours in 1907, showing the gable on 106 and the bell-cote on 108 and in the left foreground the gate to Placelands.

THE POST OFFICE BUILDING, London Road

This building, a little further along London Road, is the only purpose-built Post Office East Grinstead has ever had. It was commissioned in 1895 and completed the following year to a Ministry of Works design similar in style and materials (non-local red brick and cream terra-cotta) to other post offices of the period. The builders were a non-local firm, Messrs Davies & Leaney, with internal work undertaken by town tradesmen. Beside the lofty main hall was the telegraph instrument room and behind that the sky-lit sorting room, still used for its original purpose at the time of writing. An inspection chamber permitted undetected surveillance if there was cause for suspicion. Various other offices occupied the first floor and above them was a four-room caretaker's flat.

The opening by the Postmaster General, the Duke of Norfolk, on 16 September 1896 was preceded by a procession from the station led by a band through decorated streets and then a banquet. In the evening the Cycling Club organised a lantern parade of decorated bicycles and a 'battle of confetti', after which a dinner was held for the post office staff.

In the 20th century a telephone exchange was installed upstairs, until a purpose-built one was created on another site in 1965. By then the counter-office seemed cramped and crowded, with its steps an inconvenience to many. A few years ago, in line with national policy, the counter business was at last transferred to Forbuoys' shop, while all other post office functions remained. Finally, early

The Post Office in 1903 or soon after, with buildings familiar today either side of it, yet everything shown on the opposite side of the road has gone through redevelopment or enemy action.

in 2005, it was definitely announced that the sorting office would move to the Charlwoods Industrial Estate. The new location was deplored as inconvenient for the public and there was anxiety about what might become of this prime town-centre site and whether we would lose one of the most pleasing façades on the architecturally undistinguished side of the street. There had earlier been attempts to have it listed but one must acknowledge it is not of sufficient merit.

THE NEW TOWN MUSEUM, Cantelupe Road

The path westwards along the front of the churchyard, originally the northern edge of the High Street, leads into the former portland of 39 High Street [46] and to the new Town Museum, still in building at the time of writing.

Serious proposals for a museum in East Grinstead were first made in 1917 but nothing happened till a room was made available in the church tower in 1925. With no more security than a 'gentleman's agreement', the highly miscellaneous collection was dispersed in the late 1950s with no written records. A local history exhibition mounted by the East Grinstead Society in 1972 prompted re-invigorated calls for a proper museum. On local government re-organisation in 1974 the newly created Town Council offered the society accommodation for the purpose at East Court [8].

The museum opened there in 1976, run entirely by volunteers. A trust was created to run it in 1983 and it became fully registered under the national scheme in 2002.

This site, then home to an architecturally undistinguished saleroom for the market that stretched back to the end of the adjoining office-block, was acquired in 1997 for a permanent museum. Following the failure of a first application to the Heritage Lottery Fund, a new bid for a purpose-built, energy-efficient, low-maintenance building and a professionally qualified salaried curator resulted in an 83.6 per cent grant in December 2003. This attracted grants from Mid Sussex District Council and other bodies and a variety of donations and fund-raising events. Building began in March 2005. None of this would have been possible without generous financial help and unstinting assistance of other kinds from the Town Council at every stage. The building has been designed by Martin Green Associates of Horsted Keynes.

The Museum Society, founded in 1983 to support the museum, issues a thrice-yearly newsletter and *East Grinstead*

Museum Compass, a periodical devoted to reliable articles on the museum's collections and the history of East Grinstead and the neighbouring parishes in Kent, Surrey and Sussex, as well as having a full programme of activities for members.

South (top) and west elevations of the new museum, as prepared by MGArchitects in 2005.

SPRINGVALE, 72 Moat Road

From the far end of Cantelupe Road a path behind the houses in Christopher Road leads to a footbridge over the relief road into Moat Road. Beyond Moat Pond, Springvale stands on the opposite side of the road to which the pond gave name, a handsome example of the polychrome brickwork fashionable when it was built, sometimes termed 'streaky bacon'.

72 Moat Road c.1906, photographed from behind the hedge on the opposite side of the road by Arthur Harding.

It was begun in 1880 as a replacement for the town's first cottage hospital, which had closed in 1874. All expenses of building and equipping were borne by Dr C.H. Gatty of Felbridge – not a medical doctor but a Doctor of Laws. For reasons no longer known, it did not open until March 1887. By December it had been closed and all the contents sold.

In May that year Dr Gatty had withdrawn from the presidency of the Town Band because it had taken part without authorisation in the spontaneous celebration by some 3,000 townsfolk of the judge's verdict that the former workhouse site in London Road was the property of the parishioners. Closing the hospital was probably therefore to express his disapproval of the uninhibited demonstration in the streets and also of the tarring of the fountain [33] given by the Rev. C.W.P. Crawfurd, in apparent retaliation for his comparable withdrawal of support from the band.

The 1891 census found Gatty's former coachman John Betchley residing in the premises as caretaker, with a 65-year-old lodger living on her own means. Ten years later his lodger was a retired clergyman with means of his own. John Betchley continued to live there and let apartments to gentlefolk until the mid-1930s, apparently very profitably. His kinsman Sidney Betchley was a local benefactor, for instance part-funding the clocktower [51].

In March 1939, in preparation for war, 72 Moat Road was converted to be a new health centre and clinic, most appropriately in view of its origin. It soon became the focal point for first aid services, for example receiving the first casualties from the bombing of the Whitehall [49] in 1943. After the war it continued as the centre for services for expectant mothers, for babies, and for children referred by school doctors, dentists and oculists.

Finally it took on its current role of community mental health centre, with a new name, Springvale, derived from a spring in the grounds.

POELS COURT, Moat Road

*Poels Court from the north in June 2005,
photographed for this book by S.R. Kerr.*

studio of A. Basebe, a photographer, portrait- and miniature-painter, also at South Kensington, who had exhibited at the Royal Academy.

The house's most famous owners were Mr and Mrs Richard Powell, who had taken over by 1916 and stayed until the 1950s. He was related to Lord Baden-Powell, the founder of the Scouts and Guides, and renamed the house Poels to promote correct pronunciation of the family name; the first syllable like the 'po' in poetry, not the 'pow' in power. Older locals still remember the elegant open Bentley car in which he made his stately progress.

But his wife, Dora, was more distinguished, for as a young woman in Wolverhampton she became a friend of Sir Edward Elgar, who dedicated to her the tenth of his Enigma Variations, 'Dorabella', his nickname for her. Before coming here she had been a pupil of Sir Henry Wood, the founder of the 'Proms'. In East Grinstead Dora Powell founded the still-flourishing Operatic Society in 1922, co-founded the music club and ran a choir. She also organised the annual tennis tournaments on the Ship Street courts that drew many pre-Wimbledon players. Mrs Powell died in a local nursing home in 1964 in her 90th year, by which time the old house had been demolished. The name of the flats that replaced it is a permanent reminder of one of East Grinstead's most notable residents.

Beyond Springvale, round the bend of Moat Road, adjoining King George's Field, is an unremarkable-seeming block of flats, Poels Court. It stands on the site of one of the first houses to be built in the road, Oak Croft, in existence by 1873. Its first occupant, presumably the person for whom it was built, was George Searle Head, of the family whose bank failed in 1892. By 1885 it was the home and

THE OLD CONVENT

The convent from the north-west early in the 20th century (photographed by William Page and issued by him as a postcard).

Approached along St Agnes Road, opposite Poels Court stands the Old Convent, 'an example of Gothic Revival architecture which no other country in Europe can equal' in the words of Peter F. Anson, the historian of Anglican religious communities. It was built for the Society of St Margaret, founded in 1854 by the Rev. John Mason Neale, the Warden of Sackville College [16], to nurse the sick poor in their own homes within a radius of 25 miles. It is often considered

the masterpiece of its architect, George Edmund Street, who also designed Neale's tomb in the parish churchyard. The foundation stone was laid in 1865 and the work was far enough advanced in 1870 for it to open, though the complex was not completed until 1909 under Street's son. Built of sandstone from Hackenden, a little to the north-east, it included a quadrangle, refectory, lofty chapel and tower, making a noble and impressive group, somewhat austere but given warmth by the colour and texture of local stone and tiles.

It was the mother house of an order that spread to Scotland, the U.S.A., South Africa and Ceylon, as well as working in various parts of England and in East Grinstead itself. The sisters have always adapted to meeting new needs that no-one else has taken up and dropped work when it is no longer needed or other bodies can do it better.

By the 1970s, as the sisterhood's numbers and requirements changed, it had become too large and too expensive to maintain. The sisters moved to a modern building in the grounds and, after a financially unsuccessful spell housing their girls' school, it was sold and converted to superior and characterful private dwellings. It is therefore not open to the public but can be glimpsed in its different aspects from the path from Mount Noddy to Hackenden Lane and along the unmade stretch of that road to the bridge over the railway. Its national importance was recognised by grade 1 listing in 1981 and an obligation on the residents to maintain the disused and empty chapel.

By 2005 the remaining sisters were few and aging and so, always realistic, they decided, after 150 years in East Grinstead, to move to a small house in Uckfield. At the time of writing their new convent here has been demolished for replacement by housing, such are the pressures on any potential sites.

Sister Ermenild, youngest daughter of the founder, Mother Superior 1902-32.

Interior of the chapel early in the 20th century showing the high altar.

THE GATEHOUSE AND DOVECOTES, Dunnings Road

Dovecotes (left) and the Gatehouse (right) in 1907

From the parish church, across the High Street and down Hermitage Lane beside the *Dorset Arms* [27], it is a pleasant walk to the junction of Herontye Drive, Ship Street and Dunnings Road, where this picturesque building stands. It dates from the early 1860s, when it was built by Mr Charles Chevall Tooke of Hurst-an-Clays as part of a scheme to convert the public road which ran past his door into access drives. He laid out an extension of Ship Street from Hermitage Lane to where the tennis club now is, building a stone wall alongside and lodges at either end, both of which are still standing.

The lodge at this new top entrance is now called Field Cottage, and, much extended, houses a doctor's surgery. The lower drive passed under the arch through the lodge illustrated here, with a functional dovecote in its circular tower. The stones for all the work were quarried at the site of the former workhouse in London Road, which Mr Tooke had bought in 1862 and sold again in 1864.

When the Hurst-an-Clays estate was sold for housing development in 1958, the space under the arch was turned into extra accommodation and the building divided into two dwellings, the Gatehouse and Dovecotes. They were listed grade 2 in 1979 on the suggestion of the East Grinstead Society.

ST BARNABAS'S CHURCH, Dunnings Road

St Barnabas's in the 1950s or '60s.

Lady Musgrave, an American whose Hurst-an-Clays estate ran down the western side of Dunnings Road, was concerned at the harmful potential of intoxicating drink, and so in 1913 she made available a barn as an alcohol-free meeting place for men. Within two years it was 'the Sunnyside Mission', with services conducted by the clergy of the parish church for the spiritual welfare of all residents in the area, perhaps consciously rivalling Zion's enterprise.

In the 1920s the barn was replaced by a green-painted 'tin' church, and the then vicar of East Grinstead, Dr Golding-Bird, decided it needed an appropriate dedication. Characteristically he chose St Barnabas, in punning allusion to the building it replaced. Thirty years later there was talk of closure because St Barnabas's was not paying its way, but the core congregation remained faithful and, as new housing developments encroached behind both sides of Dunnings Road, the church flourished again.

The existing building then proved increasingly worn-out and inadequate and so it was replaced by the existing prefabricated purpose-built church-cum-hall, dedicated by the Bishop of Horsham on 18 July 1975. In addition to a service every Sunday and Thursday, it currently hosts cubs, scouts and brownies, a mothers' and toddlers' group and a ladies' circle and acts as a polling station in elections, providing a focal point for a community which, thanks to the steep hill, still retains a certain separation from the rest of the town.

Almost at the bottom of Dunnings Road, on the same side as the Gatehouse and Dovecotes, is St Barnabas's church.

Development of the Sunnyside estate here – Stockwell, Morton, Coronation and Forest View Roads, leading eastwards off the opposite side of Dunnings Road – was under way in 1892. In due course shops appeared and in 1904 a 'mission' under the auspices of Zion Chapel [42].

OLD HOLLYBUSH FARM,
5–6 Standen Cottages (TQ 390356)

Beyond St Barnabas's, past Dunnings Mill, and then straight on up Frampost Hollow one comes on the left to the turning for Standen [78], which brings one first to Old Hollybush Farm.

When Philip Webb created Standen on a new site in the 1890s he took care to integrate into the complex the medieval cottages which had been Great Hollybush Farm and to respect their features in his main design. The roof and southern and eastern fronts remain visible to visitors, with typical vernacular brickwork and tile-hanging and a glimpse of the medieval rafters. Much of the original timber-framing remains within. It is a typical yeoman's house of about 1450 with a central hall, originally open to the roof, a private first-floor chamber (a solar) at the 'upper' end and service rooms at the other, separated from the hall by a cross-passage with outside doors at each end. Some of the original roof-timbers are still intact but the northern end was rebuilt in the 17th century. The hall was floored over in the 16th century to create more first-floor accommodation and a brick chimney was inserted in the first half of the seventeenth.

The first definite reference to this farm is in 1597, when it was known as Holmwood, a name which, usually as Homewood, can be traced back to the early 12th century and also became a local surname.

Today the building is listed grade 2 and cared for by the National Trust but, as a private residence, it is not open to the public.

Old Hollybush Farm, right, and Webb's entrance gateway and service wing linking it to Standen, left, c.1990 (photograph by D. Pocock).

STANDEN
(TQ 390356)

Standen, one of East Grinstead's four grade 1 buildings, is a national treasure of the Arts and Crafts movement. Thanks to the generosity of Miss Helen Beale, its last private owner, in bequeathing it to the National Trust in 1973, lest it be ruined by unsympathetic newcomers, we can all enjoy the house and contents, the garden and the views over Weir Wood reservoir to the slopes of Ashdown Forest.

As a small child, Miss Beale saw the house, designed and decorated by the architect Philip Webb, being built from 1892 to 1894 for her father, the London solicitor James Beale. Contemporary furnishings by William Morris and his followers, including tapestries worked by Mrs Beale and her daughters, were lovingly cared for. Very little therefore needed to be done to recreate the house's original appearance, while the contents have been enriched by extra items of the same style and period.

The National Trust justly claims it as the best example in this country of an Arts and Crafts house open to the public and a perfect illustration of that movement's emphasis on hand craftsmanship and traditional materials. Webb naturally integrated Old Hollybush Farm [77] into his design and used sandstone from the site, hand-made bricks from Keymer and Horsham, Wealden tiles and weatherboarding. A functional tower for the water-tanks holds the whole complex together visually.

The name Standen, meaning stony valley and first recorded in Domesday Book in 1086, was actually that of a small farmhouse a little further south, inhabited by agricultural labourers by the time the Beales acquired it. It was demolished in c.1896 but the Beales were careful to preserve not only the name but also the ancient local pronunciation, with the stress on 'den', a tradition that deserves to be respected today as much as the house and grounds they created.

Standen from the south-east, c.1900, photographed by William Page and issued by him as a postcard.

SAINT HILL
(TQ 383358)

The present house, of local sandstone, is partly as put up between 1788 and 1792 for Gibbs Crawfurd, M.P. for Queenborough, whose family had acquired the estate in *c.*1733 not long after moving from Scotland. His descendants still have a silver trowel inscribed 'to Henry Pocock, 24 Aug. 1792'. Pocock, an East Grinstead stonemason, must have been the designer of the house, working from pattern books in the custom of the time.

In 1859 Robert Crawfurd sold Saint Hill to William Thomas Berger, a prosperous starch manufacturer who was the chief financial backer of Hudson Taylor, the famous pioneer missionary in China. Berger made provision at Saint Hill for training young men to go out to assist him and also built a school-cum-chapel at Saint Hill Green, now a private house.

In 1890 a later owner, Edgar March Crookshank, pulled down part of Saint Hill and enlarged it to become the main building we see today. He was the founder of the first bacteriological laboratory in England, at King's College Hospital, and the unsuccessful Unionist candidate for East Grinstead in the 1906 election.

By the mid-20th century the Maharajah of Jaipur had Saint Hill. In his time George Chatham, to his fellows 'the finest cat burglar of the century', opened the safe with a foot-long custom-made key and stole £80,000.

L. Ron Hubbard, the founder of Scientology, acquired the property in 1958. He added other buildings, some inspired by Tonbridge Castle. Scientology members still proudly care for the grade 2 building and open it every day for visits.

Saint Hill from the air in 1975.

Beyond the Standen access road, a little way west of Saint Hill Green on the road to Hazelden crossroads, though hardly visible from it, stands Saint Hill Manor, as it is now called. The best views are actually distant ones from some of the public footpaths in the area.

The house on the site has frequently been rebuilt, each time more grandly than before, but it was never a manor house, for there was no manor of Saint Hill. The name, first recorded as Saint Hill in 1656, was originally Sand Hill, traceable from the late 13th century.

FOREST ROW VILLAGE HALL

At the junction of all the roads that enter Forest Row stands its handsome Village Hall, given by Henry Ray Freshfield of Kidbrooke [82] and his family in memory of his 14-year-old grandson, also Henry, who died in 1891. The architect was J.M. Brydon, well known for municipal and government buildings, the builder Job Luxford, who put up nearly all the significant buildings in the area, and the cost about £2,000. It was opened on 4 November 1892 by the M.P. for East Grinstead, the Hon. A.E. Gathorne Hardy.

Henry Freshfield senior died in 1895. On the day after his funeral, 14 February, the hall burnt down, apparently from the overheating of a flue above the kitchen, leaving only the shell of the front, although much of the rear was saved. Mrs Freshfield and her son Douglas speedily re-engaged Brydon and Luxford to rebuild it as before and it re-opened on 17 November.

The south front of the Village Hall at the start of the 20th century.

The façade, with sandstone for the ground floor, tile-hanging for the upper, and brick chimneys at the ends, deliberately echoes local vernacular buildings but with the addition of a central porch with lush plaster decoration. Timber-framing above the porch and in the gables continues the vernacular theme but with a little lantern and spirelet centrally placed over the main hall. Inside there was a parish room to the left at the front and a caretaker's residence on two floors along the eastern side. A soup kitchen operated in winter and a working men's club was formed in 1894. Three years later a committee took over management from the Freshfields.

During the First World War the army occupied the building. In 1929 it was enlarged to provide an extra hall at the rear. Recently this room was renamed after the late Peter Griffits, who for nearly four decades had voluntarily served Forest Row by holding office in some thirty local organisations, serving on the parish and district councils, and fulfilling a variety of roles at the parish church [83]. In 1993 the parish council office moved from this grade 2 listed building to the new community centre [81].

FOREST ROW COMMUNITY CENTRE, Hartfield Road

The main building of Forest Row's community centre, a little way east of the Village Hall, was erected in 1851 and opened in 1852 as an elementary school. It was associated with the National Society, an organisation founded to provide education for the poor in accordance with the principles of the Church of England and designed to cater for 200 children drawn from an area of 6½ by 3¼ miles with a poor population of about 1,400.

The driving force was Forest Row's first vicar, the Rev. Joseph Atkins Beckett, who raised funds by appealing for donations and publishing a volume of his sermons. Fees for a labourer's child were twopence a week, for a tradesman's or farmer's fourpence. Soon as many as thirty children walked to it every day from East Grinstead, where there was nothing comparable until 1861 [5].

There was also a teacher's house, a storeroom in which was converted to a kitchen in 1926 when the school became the first in Sussex to provide a midday meal for children who could not go home for one. A canteen was opened two years later.

In 1933 the Memorial Hall alongside, to be used for domestic science and carpentry lessons, was funded by the Hambro family of Kidbrooke [82] to commemorate Mrs Hambro's death by drowning. Further additions in that year allowed the over-11s from Hartfield to be accommodated.

In January 1943 the playground was machine-gunned at lunch-time but mercifully there were no casualties. During the flying bomb threat in 1944 a boy with a whistle was stationed on the roof to give warning.

As the 20th century drew to a close, the present primary school was built further along Hartfield Road and in 1993 the parish council bought the old premises and converted them to a community centre, with meeting rooms, kitchen, library, council office and other facilities. The little stone pillar formerly by the horse-trough in the Square was re-erected in the grounds.

The Community Centre from the east-north-east in June 2005, photographed for this book by S.R. Kerr.

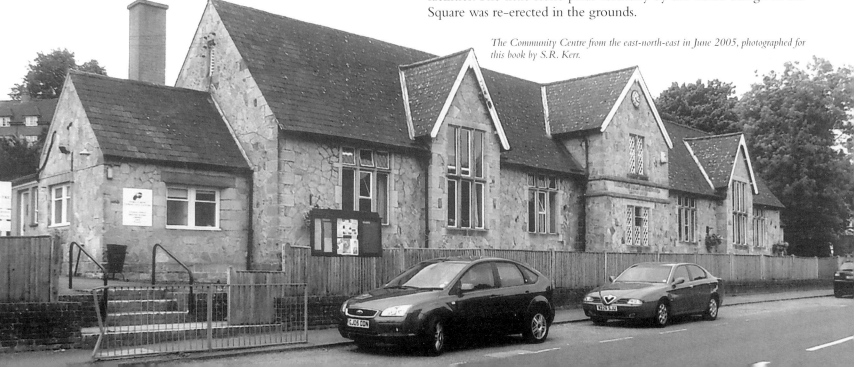

KIDBROOKE (MICHAEL HALL SCHOOL), Forest Row

A path turning left off Hartfield Road opposite the *Foresters* leads across the A22 to Gilham Lane, off which a path on the left leads towards and past Kidbrooke.

In 1733 William Nevill, Lord Abergavenny, obtained an Act of Parliament to purchase the land on which to build the house. The site was marshy, taking its name at least as early as the 15th century from the stream running through it. The house, in local sandstone, consisted of a central block of five bays on two floors with service wings north and south. The stable block alongside has a clock with the date 1736.

Charles Abbot, Baron Colchester, in 1817.

In 1803 the Nevills returned to their ancestral home at Eridge and sold Kidbrooke to Charles Abbot, who had become Speaker of the House of Commons the previous year. On retiring in 1816 he was ennobled as Baron Colchester. Between 1806 and 1809 he engaged the celebrated landscape gardener Humphry Repton to redesign the grounds and the architect George Dance junior in 1815 to add to the south front the colonnade visible in the photograph. The central block remains virtually unchanged.

Inevitably the owners of Kidbrooke acted as unofficial squires of Forest Row, supporting all worthwhile village activities. After the Colchesters they included Henry Ray Freshfield, of the solicitors to the Bank of England, Lewes Pendarves Kekewich, Sir James Horlick, of the bedtime drink, and Ronald Olaf Hambro. In 1939 the estate was sold to the Alliance Assurance Company, evacuated from London, which put up 15 huts in the grounds.

At the end of the war the Steiner Waldorf school Michael Hall moved in from Minehead, establishing itself as an influential presence in the Forest Row area and attracting other Steiner enterprises to follow it here. Despite the high costs, and other priorities, the school manfully does its utmost to restore and maintain worthily its fine grade 2 listed building. At the same time it has improved its facilities with purpose-built outbuildings in the distinctive Steiner style, including a theatre seating 700 constructed in 1980.

The west and south fronts of Kidbrooke in the 1920s.

HOLY TRINITY CHURCH, Forest Row

Forest Row's parish church stands accessibly at the road junction diagonally opposite the Village Hall [80] on a site where cock-fighting and boxing took place until the church displaced their ethos with the more wholesome influences of religion and morality.

The village of Forest Row started developing in the 14th century, a hamlet in the parish of East Grinstead. The nearby chapel at Brambletye, more convenient than the church in the town, was closed in the 1540s. As usual in such situations, religious dissenters established themselves in Forest Row in the 17th and 18th centuries, long before the Church of England made better provision for the growing village.

An Anglican church there was first suggested in 1833 by the curate of East Grinstead, the Rev. Christopher Nevill, who devoted most of his time to the Forest Row area. Lord Gage gave the site, funds were raised and William Moseley designed the building, which was consecrated in 1836 together with its burial ground. There was seating for 436, 100 rentable spaces, the rest free benches of more basic form. This proved insufficient, so in 1850 a Chichester architect, Joseph Butler, inserted a gallery, giving 365 free seats and 116 not free. A small vestry was added at the same time.

In 1877, when a side-aisle designed by Herbert Green was added, the gallery was removed and new seating installed, all free. Stained glass, new furnishings and memorials steadily offset the austerity of the building, whose most elaborate feature had been its barn-type roof.

In 1954 a legacy from Harry Neal of Legsheath Farm financed an extension, a much-needed Church Hall. Five years later Sir Harry and Lady Sinderson paid for an automatic eight-note system to replace the two old bells. This meant an end to tolling to announce the deaths of parishioners and their funerals. A clock had already been installed in 1859, a useful amenity for the whole village at whose centre the church stands, not merely geographically but also in its continuing involvement with so many aspects of the life of Forest Row.

The church from the east in 1933.

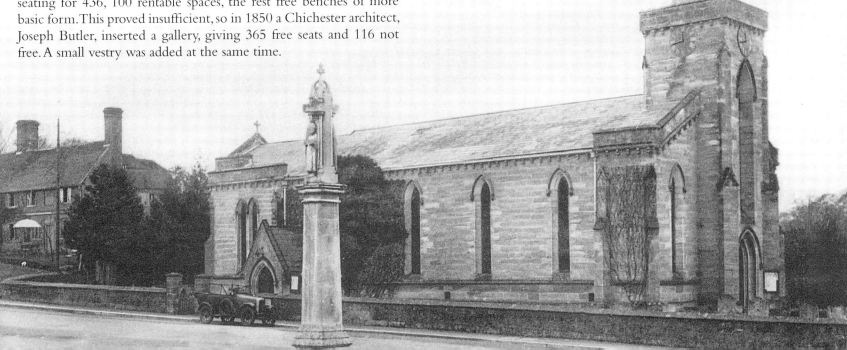

THE SWAN, Forest Row

Completing the trio of public buildings at the central road junction, the *Swan* began as a small two-up two-down timber-framed dwelling put up between about 1570 and 1630. About a hundred years later a stone chimney was added at the northern end and the building was extended at the southern end. The new part was taller but still timber-framed, with carpentry that has been pronounced very good. This extension probably coincides with its becoming an inn, at first called the *Yew Tree* but by 1775 the *Swan*. It was, and is, admirably positioned to have a good passing trade as well as serving the resident population.

A further extension to the south had been created by 1834 when the present stone front was added to the whole building, designed by William Moseley who was next responsible for the church [83]. By then it was the only inn in the village and hosted various public events, including monthly sittings of the magistrates. It was also the social centre of Forest Row. On 25 June 1826, fair day, the landlord, John Hoare, organised sports and fireworks. In 1844 his successor, Jonathan Clapson, erected an arch of evergreens outside for the arrival of Lord Ellenborough when he came to stay with Lord Colchester at Kidbrooke [82]. No doubt he was also responsible for his lordship's reception at the bridge by villagers with flags and music, and no doubt also the escorts returned to the *Swan* for refreshment once Lord Ellenborough had been safely delivered to his host.

In 2005 the *Swan* was converted from a public house to a 'Mountain Range' restaurant, without changing its name.

The Swan in 1907 with the churchyard wall in the foreground.

Brambletye Castle is about a third of a mile north-west of the centre of Forest Row and most easily reached by a footpath that starts between two shops on the western side of the Square. It is not a castle, however, but the ruins of a mansion built in 1631 but abandoned and ruined by the end of the century.

It was not the first building at Brambletye. It replaced one on a moated site nearby, and in the 11th century Brambletye was the principal settlement in the East Grinstead area. The name, which means enclosure or common or open field marked by brambles, is pronounced with the stress on the last syllable.

Using local sandstone and in the latest architectural fashion, the structure whose remains we see now was built for Sir Henry Compton, whose initials with those of his wife and the date survive on the central tower. It is claimed that a later owner, Sir James Richards, had to flee the country, after which it was uninhabited, valued only as a ready-made source of building materials. Thus from 1747 to 49 several loads of stones from Brambletye were bought for repairs to the bridge at Edenbridge.

By the end of that century, however, the ruins were regarded as romantic, hence no doubt the name Brambletye Castle, first found in 1795. In 1826 Horace Smith published a novel like those of Sir Walter Scott, *Brambletye House*, which was widely read and brought more tourists. Although destruction ceased, the ruins could still be scrambled over until the 1950s.

In the 1920s and '30s the only room not open to the sky served as home to a local character, Jimmy Hobbs, who had been born in about 1855. By 1949, though, the structure had been scheduled

A painting of Brambletye Castle in 1809 (reproduced as a postcard by Arthur Harding in the early 20th century).

as an ancient monument and in due course it was fenced off with railings.

By following the farm drive to the A22 and crossing it to a steeply climbing footpath one can reach Ashurst Wood. Turning left off the drive onto the Forest Way, the former railway from East Grinstead to Tunbridge Wells, one can regain the town two miles away to the north-west.

ST DUNSTAN'S CHURCH, Ashurst Wood

St Dunstan's church is in the centre of Ashurst Wood, within sight of the war memorial, where there is a bus stop.

When the village's first place of worship, a room on the common seating 80 founded by Zion Chapel in East Grinstead [42], was threatened with closure in 1855, it was purchased for £50 by the Rev. Benjamin Slight, a retired Congregationalist minister living in the town, and reinvigorated. It soon proved too small and so the building illustrated here was erected on the opposite side of the road and opened on 11 October 1859 with seating for 220. Only the framework of the spire was in place, however, and violent wind on 5 November felled it. Some saw this as divine judgement on having such a feature on a Nonconformist place of worship.

The chapel flourished for nearly a century but in 1953 proved unable to fund a full-time minister or find anyone to take on the post until the Rev. Norman S. Jenkinson from Oxted agreed to serve part-time four years later.

Numbers continued to decline, however, and in October 1973 the chapel closed, though it was still used for Sunday School and meetings of local organisations. Planning permission was obtained in 1974 for replacement by a house and the Village Community Action Group got permission for alternative use, but the remaining members of the congregation wanted the Church of England to take it over. The latter had long found its existing church, on the A22 by the *Three Crowns* [88], inadequate, poorly located and noisy. The Anglicans therefore bought the Congregational chapel for £8,750 in April 1977, rededicating it in September 1979 to their previous church's patron, St Dunstan, Archbishop of Canterbury AD 959–88 and associated with Mayfield in Sussex. Their former church is now a private house.

Today the 'new' St Dunstan's serves not only for worship, as part of the parish of Forest Row, but also as a well-used meeting place with a room housing the office of Ashurst Wood Parish Council.

The 'new' St Dunstan's from the south in June 2005, photographed for this book by S.R. Kerr.

ASHURST WOOD ABBEY, Hammerwood Road

Off Hammerwood Road as it leaves the built-up area of Ashurst Wood beyond the church, Ashurst Wood Abbey, as it is now called, has had a colourful history, beginning in 1846 when John Epps, a homoeopathic doctor, religious Nonconformist and political radical, made his first purchase of land here. Fifteen years after acquiring that 'truly exquisite spot', he built, on the site of Pawleys Farm, a house commanding a panoramic view of Forest Row and Ashdown Forest which he named the Yews. Because he was associated with Epps's cocoa, irreverent locals dubbed it 'Cocoa Castle'. He died in 1869.

By 1887 the house had been renamed Yewhurst and was owned by people called Bell. Between 1888 and 91 a grander replacement was constructed by the Forest Row builder James Waters, perhaps for Edwin Dunning who was in residence by 1895. Around the turn of the century it was acquired by Sir Abe Bailey, a South African diamond tycoon and politician and also a keen sportsman. He gave £1,000 to the Queen Victoria Hospital [9] and once brought his country's cricket team to play in East Grinstead.

In 1919 the premises of St Andrew's prep school at Southborough burnt down and its headmaster, the Rev. Reginald Alfred Bull, moved it to Yewhurst and added a chapel. During the Second World War it received and amalgamated with another prep school, the Abbey, evacuated from Beckenham where it had been founded in about 1870. The newcomer's name was given to the joint venture.

After the school closed in 1969 the premises were bought by a somewhat eccentric humanist named Jean (pronounced Gene) Straker, a photographer of the female nude from Soho famous for challenging the censors. He renamed his new home Ashurst Wood Abbey and founded there the Ashurst Wood Academy of the Arts for free expression in creativity and discussion. He also took a leading part in promoting a sense of community in the village. On his death in 1984 the buildings were converted into flats.

One cannot, therefore, get a close look, but there are impressive views of the pale-coloured building on the brow of the hill from the slopes above Forest Row.

A corner of Yewhurst early in the 20th century published by W. 'Avory' [correctly Avery] of Ashurst Wood Post Office as a postcard.

THE THREE CROWNS, Ashurst Wood

At the other end of Hammerwood Road and alongside the A22, formerly the main road from London to Lewes and Brighton, the *Three Crowns* was built on the edge of Ashurst Wood Common where the original village nucleus began to form in the 16th and 17th centuries. It was thus well-placed for business, even when the 'Brambletye Bends' bypassing the village in 1826 took the new road behind the house.

It is first recorded in 1767 as the *Crowns*, when Michael Bromley bequeathed it to his grandson Michael Cufftree. Bromley had taken the premises in 1734, described as a carpenter, but on his marriage in 1721 he had called himself a victualler. A victualler supplied food and drink for consumption on the premises, so the building might well have been an inn before 1767. By the time Cufftree gave it up in 1786 it was referred to as the *Three Crowns*, probably a more precise version of the earlier name. There is unlikely to have been any special significance in the choice of such a common inn-name. In 1861 it was taken over by Charles Absalom, an East Grinstead brewer who was buying up local licensed premises. His holdings eventually passed to the Southdown and East Grinstead Breweries, then to the Brighton brewers Tamplins, and from them to the national concern Watneys.

Coaches at the Three Crowns, c. *1929-33.*

With the coming of charabancs and motor-coaches, its roadside position served the *Three Crowns* well, as a half-way relief and refreshment stop between London and the coast. When this traffic declined, the enormous pre-war lavatory block was converted into a short-lived in-house brewery in 1983. More recently the sign has been repainted to show three crowns of different types rather than the usual identical ones.

LITTLE SHOVELSTRODE HALL,
Holtye Road, East Grinstead (TQ 414394)

Little Shovelstrode Hall, beside the A264 about a mile and a half north-east of East Grinstead parish church as the crow flies, looks from the outside a typical 17th-century framed building of no particular interest. When investigated, however, by the late Peter Gray it proved to possess enough original timbers inside to show that it was a mid-14th-century hall-house, extensively reconstructed in the 1600s and therefore one of East Grinstead's oldest buildings.

Documentary research has shown that it stands on the site of the Celrestvis of Domesday Book, indicating a history of settlement going back some 950 years, maybe longer. In 1066 Celrestvis was held by someone named Aelmer, about whom nothing seems to be known. After the Norman conquest it was granted to Ansfrid, along with three other local properties.

Since then it has had a number of names. In the 16th century it was known as Yealdalls, after a family who had lived there since at least 1296. An alternative name was Lesser or Little Shovelstrode, but by the 19th century it was again being called after its occupants, Goodwins or sometimes Betchleys. When a large house named Orchards was built nearby in 1907 for Sir Samuel Cunard, the shipping magnate, it became Orchards Cottage, but recently its older name was revived, as Little Shovelstrode Hall.

The terms Lesser or Little were applied to distinguish it from the larger holding generally known simply as Shovelstrode, north of Ashurst Wood, which also appears in Domesday Book. Its name is given there as Calvrestot, meaning marshy ground by the slope, of which Celrestvis is another form and Shovelstrode the final version of later rationalisation.

Today Little Shovelstrode Hall is listed grade 2.

Little Shovelstrode Hall in November 1995 (photographed for this book by S.R. Kerr).

HAMMERWOOD PARK
(TQ 442387)

Further along the A264, down a lane beside Hammerwood church, is a house recently promoted to grade 1. Its core dates from 1792, when 28-year-old Benjamin Henry Latrobe was asked by the equally young John Sperling to design a house near Ashdown Forest. Inspired by the earliest classical architecture, that of Greece in the sixth century BC, Latrobe boldly defied contemporary preferences for the fifth-century style and produced a design that was ahead of its time. At Hammerwood Lodge, as it was called until the 1920s, he did not follow classical models slavishly but showed originality and great skill. The interiors are spacious and the site commands a remarkably unspoilt southern vista beyond the watercourse that in the mid-17th century powered Bower Forge.

Bower is still the name of the 16th-century farmhouse adjacent to Hammerwood Park, traceable back to 1288 and meaning house or room. It was Sperling who coined Hammerwood as an appropriate and romantic name for his new home.

Latrobe developed his skills two years later at Ashdown House [91] and then in the U.S.A., where his principal buildings are the Bank of Pennsylvania in Philadelphia, Baltimore cathedral and the south wing (only) of the Capitol in Washington.

In 1795 Sperling had to return to Essex to care for his father. Three generations of the Dorrien Magens family of bankers owned Hammerwood until the mid-1860s when they sold to another banker, Oswald Augustus Smith. One of these families made additions to the house. Both took a leading part in local public life. J. Dorrien Magens, for example, was chairman of the East Grinstead Railway Company [67] and Mr and Mrs Smith financed the nearby church and school as well as a new hospital in 1887 to replace the one Dr Gatty had just closed [72] and other philanthropic work in the town.

The next owner, the Rev. George Ferris Whidborne, allowed Hammerwood to be used for disabled soldiers in the First World War, after which it was temporarily the home of St Andrew's preparatory school before it settled in Ashurst Wood [87]. It remained a private residence until 1973, apart from being turned over to the military when the Second World War broke out. Special Operations Executive personnel were ferried between France and Hammerwood in light aircraft to rest between missions. In 1973 a rock group called Led Zeppelin acquired the house but let it become derelict.

It was rescued in June 1982 by 21-year-old David Pinnegar, thanks to a timely inheritance. With his mother he initiated a long programme of loving restoration, still not complete, to high standards but not always without controversy, gathering friends and supporters and opening to the public on a limited number of summer afternoons.

Hammerwood Park from the south-west, c.1900, photographed by William Page and issued by him as a postcard.

ASHDOWN HOUSE, Forest Row
(TQ 445358)

An exquisite morsel', 'a gem of a house ... all Ionic feminine grace' and 'very perfect indeed' are descriptions of Ashdown House by, respectively, an American newspaper correspondent in 1805, John Julius, Viscount Norwich in the last century, and Professor Nikolaus Pevsner in 1965.

It was designed in 1794 for John Trayton Fuller by B.H. Latrobe, two years after his only other English building, Hammerwood Lodge [90], and two years before emigrating to America, where he stayed until his death in 1820. He built it on the crown of a hill commanding magnificent views, adjoining the front of the existing late 16th-century Lavertye farmhouse. It is a three-storey, almost square, block inspired by the architecture of fifth-century BC Greece. The comparatively modest-sized house created by Latrobe gained a kitchen wing in Victorian times and the estate remained the Fullers' property until 1910.

The south front of Ashdown House in the first half of the 20th century.

In 1886, however, it was leased to Connaught House School, which had been founded in Brighton in 1843 and had already prepared the sons of many British and foreign noblemen for the leading public schools or officer training for the armed forces.

The school was soon renamed Ashdown House. During the 20th century new buildings were added and the amenities upgraded but the core is still Latrobe's cherished house, listed grade 2 in 1955.

It is still a preparatory school today, receiving the sons, and since 1976 a smaller number of the daughters, of the eminent and preparing them for public school entrance, with many scholarships and other awards to its credit. The most notable former pupils are probably Viscount Linley and Lady Sarah Armstrong-Jones, the children of Princess Margaret and the Earl of Snowdon.

Although it is not open to the public it can be glimpsed from the top deck of buses between East Grinstead, Forest Row and Tunbridge Wells and from various footpaths in the vicinity.

DUTTON HOMESTALL (STOKE BRUNSWICK SCHOOL),
Ashurst Wood (TQ 422376)

Homestall, the original part of the complex that now houses Stoke Brunswick School, on the road north from Ashurst Wood to Shovelstrode, is probably the oldest building in our area, a fine house dating from about 1300. Originally it was a hall with aisles either side, one of which remains, including a hexagonal arcade post with a moulded capital. We do not know who had it built, and the earliest record of the name, meaning the family house of an estate, is not until 1614. Possibly it originally had a different name.

There were several alterations in Tudor times, with the arms of Elizabeth I painted on a screen, but in reverse as if copied from the wrong side of stained glass. A fine Jacobean newel staircase is another feature.

By 1845 it was divided, let to labourers and approaching decay. By 1903 it had become derelict but was saved by John Dewar, the whisky magnate. In 1933 John Dewar's nephew of the same name enlarged it by adding Dutton Hall, built with typical West Midlands ornamental framing in 1539-42 beside the River Weaver near Chester. Large lorries brought the dismantled and numbered parts to Ashurst Wood. Until then the road passed in front of the house but Dewar had a diversion built further east, known to locals ever since as Whisky Way.

During the Second World War the family made Dutton Homestall, as it was now called, a convalescent home for officers being treated at the Queen Victoria Hospital [9]. In 1958 Brunswick, a

Dutton Homestall during the Second World War, photographed by Harold Connold and issued by him as a postcard.

boys' preparatory school founded in Brighton in 1866 and moved to Haywards Heath 30 years later, took over the building. In 1963 it was joined by Stoke House, a similar school from Seaford but originally from Stoke Poges, and the names were combined. Later it became co-educational and reduced the age of entry from eight to three.

The building, listed grade 2, is, of course, not open to the public, and there are no buses along the road, but glimpses may be obtained from footpaths round about.

HERONTYE HOUSE,
East Grinstead (TQ 397372)

Now tucked away behind the award-winning 1970s housing estate to which it gives name, off Stuart Way, half a mile south of the parish church, Herontye House was built in 1912 'practically regardless of cost' for Andrew Devitt, a wealthy rubber-planter and traveller who had been born in 1850. Until 1888 the site had been occupied for a century or so by the mansion house of Brockhurst, demolished in that year and replaced by a new building off Lewes Road.

The architects, Messrs Wheeler and Godman of Horsham, intended Herontye to have an Elizabethan look, using stone from the Brockhurst estate which Devitt had purchased some time before. In the meanwhile he was acquiring old Horsham slates for the roof. The builders were H. & E. Waters of Forest Row and the masonry sub-contractors Jenner and Grynyer of East Grinstead. All the joinery was in oak, with old panels in the hall, library and corridor. An owl-house over one of the entrances was soon tenanted and a large carved heron presided over the principal entrance in obvious allusion to the name, which was as new as the house. The name must have been chosen to evoke associations with old mansions like Gravetye [96] and Brambletye [85] and like

them is pronounced with the stress on the final syllable, but why Heron was chosen is not known. The conventional interpretation of 'tye' in such place-names is enclosure but in Sussex dialect it denotes a common or a large field. Either way, it does not seem the environment herons would choose for themselves.

A lodge in keeping with the house was built on Lewes Road, where it still stands at the entrance to Herontye Drive from which Stuart Way is gained, and a winding drive was constructed under the railway (now Forest Way bridleway) through a sandstone arch.

Devitt sold Herontye in 1921 to Admiral Sir Charles Madden, Commander-in-Chief of the Atlantic fleet and eventually First Sea Lord. Five years later he sold it to the Hon. John Nivison, later Baron Glendyne. By 1975, when the estate had been sold for housing, the town council was unable to prevent Herontye's becoming the prestigious offices of an engineering company, but councillor Stuart Adams-Jones succeeded in having it listed grade 2. In 1999 it was converted back to apartments.

Admiral Sir Charles Madden, G.C.B., photographed by Hay Wrightson of New Bond Street.

The south front of Herontye when new.

KINGSCOTE STATION
(TQ 366356)

Kingscote station, just over two miles south-west of the parish church, saw its first passenger trains for 39 years on 23 April 1994 as the Bluebell Railway completed an important stage in its push towards East Grinstead. When the line closed in 1955 it was a few days earlier than intended, owing to a strike, and when the line was briefly re-opened in 1956 because the closure procedure had been flawed, Kingscote was not served because it was not one of the stations in the original Act of Parliament authorising the line.

Considering the lack of any village, the station was lavishly built and staffed and, not surprisingly, shared with Rowfant on the East Grinstead-Three Bridges line the distinction of the lowest receipts anywhere on the London, Brighton and South Coast Railway. However, it enabled nearby farmers to send milk to London, and a timberyard and sawmill were built alongside.

The architect of all the stations on this East Grinstead-Lewes line, which opened in 1882, was T.H. Myres of Preston and the contractor was Joseph Firbank. John Hoare, in his *Sussex Railway Architecture*, considers these stations to have had the most attractive design ever used by the Brighton company: brick country cottages as seen from the road, with terra-cotta ornamentation and, on the upper storey, tile-hanging typical of the Weald. We are fortunate that this fine building, which is not listed, escaped demolition, first to be a private house and then lovingly brought back into its original use by the Bluebell Railway.

The name Kingscote is no older than 1866, when Mr Joseph King built a house and named it after himself. When the line was being built that house was occupied by John Wolfe-Barry, the engineer for the line, while the navvies occupied huts nearby. No doubt that led to calling the whole area Kingscote and so adopting that name for the station.

Until the line is re-opened to East Grinstead over the viaduct [45] a dedicated bus links Kingscote station to the town centre and East Grinstead station on principal Bluebell operating days.

Kingscote station, up platform, in the 1950s.

TICKERIDGE,
near Kingscote station (TQ 365356)

Tickeridge, just round the corner from Kingscote station, is an aisled house with base-crucks, i.e. open to the roof with curved timbers extending from ground to ridge and with side-aisles giving a greater floor area. It is thus one of the oldest houses in the East Grinstead area, dated on structural and stylistic grounds to the early 14th century.

It is not, however, the first habitation on the site, for by the mid-13th century it had already given name to Simon de Teggeherugge, a carpenter who witnessed a deed granting land in the south-east of West Hoathly parish to hold a building for the rector's grain. In the Middle Ages carpenters were builders, preparing timber in their workyards for transport and erection where required. In many medieval buildings one can still see the marks on the beams that indicated how they were to be assembled. Perhaps Simon hoped to get the contract for the rector's building.

The name probably comes from the Old English words *teag*, a tye, as explained under Herontye [93], and *hrycg*, a ridge.

The adjoining farm buildings include a small weather-boarded granary on staddle stones and the longest barn in the area, 110 feet. When first built in the mid-17th century the barn consisted of five bays with double doors on either side in the centre where threshing would take place. Three further bays with their own entrance were added in the 18th century.

Today Tickeridge is a private residence, clearly visible from the road, impressive in appearance and deservedly listed grade 2.

Tickeridge from the south-west c.1906 with the railway from East Grinstead in the background, photographed by Arthur Harding.

GRAVETYE,
Vowels Lane, West Hoathly (TQ 362340)

Gravetye in 1866.

grove or copse, and stressed on the last syllable, is three hundred years older than the present building. The core of the hotel is a fine sandstone house built shortly before 1600 by Richard Infield in the most up-to-date style to proclaim the wealth he had gained from the local iron industry. It was the first in this area on the new 'double-pile' plan, i.e. two rooms deep rather than one. The location, taking over from the nearby moated enclosure, on which a 16th century house still stands, gave fine views and ensured it could be seen from distant viewpoints.

Infield's furnace was at Mill Place, a mile to the north-east, followed in the 18th century by one at Gravetye itself.

A new porch was added in about 1640 and there were alterations and a new wing in the late 19th century for Gravetye's most famous owner, the gardening writer William Robinson, who bought it in 1884. In the grounds he created world-famous gardens on the principle of a natural appearance rather than formal beds. He also planted several thousand trees to create new woods.

On his death in 1935 Robinson left the property to the state for forestry purposes, with conditions as to conservation, maintenance and public access. As a result we can walk in the

Gravetye Manor, as it is now called, off Vowels Lane about a mile south-west of Tickeridge as the crow flies, has been a high-class hotel, restaurant and country club since 1958.

In fact there never was a manor of Gravetye, and the name, meaning either an enclosure or a common or open field beside a

woods regardless of whether we can afford to patronise the hotel.

There are no passing buses and no views of the house from Vowels Lane but it shows up impressively from the road from the top of the lane to West Hoathly on which buses do run.

IMBERHORNE FARM,
East Grinstead (TQ 373384)

Imberhorne Farm lies a mile and a half west-north-west of the parish church, and is approached along a bridleway from Imberhorne Lane. The present farmhouse was built between 1808 and 11 at the behest and expense of the Duchess of Dorset, the owner of the estate, along with several outbuildings. As would be expected for a substantial farmer of the period, it is of classical design, symmetrical, elegant and dignified. The central bay projects slightly and supports a pediment, while each storey is a little less tall than the one below. There are generously proportioned sash windows and an impressive door. The foundations are of local sandstone, the walls of local grey and red bricks, and the roof of imported slate. A single-storey rear extension would have housed the scullery, wash-house and brewhouse.

Imberhorne is first recorded in *c.*1100 when it was given to Lewes Priory. Its name (stressed on the last syllable) derives from the Old English for raspberry corner, describing the site when occupied by Saxon settlers. Very probably there had been a habitation here long before, however, for the house sits alongside the prehistoric ridgeway from East Grinstead past Gullege [98] towards Crawley Down. The house thus commands fine views across open countryside towards the North Downs.

To its south is a pond, created and managed by the first builders of a homestead at the site to ensure a regular supply of fresh fish. We know that in 1295 the vicar of East Grinstead and a comrade forcibly entered the premises and took a hundred shillingsworth of the priory's fish.

Following the dissolution of Lewes Priory in 1537 Imberhorne was soon acquired by the Sackville family, in whose ownership it remained until 1872.

The farm and the manor of which it was the heart are well documented throughout this period, including detailed financial accounts for the early 19th-century house.

Imberhorne Farm in 1986, photographed by Miss R.M. Willatts.

GULLEGE,
East Grinstead (TQ 365385)

Gullege, half a mile west of Imberhorne along the bridleway, is an impressive three-bay timber-framed house with a fine Horsham stone roof and tall brick chimneys, dated by the Wealden Buildings Study Group to about 1574. It stands where the ancient ridge-top track is crossed by a sunken lane from the Crawley Down road at Felbridge that continues as a footpath across the Worth Way towards Tilkhurst. There can be little doubt that an earlier house stood on the site, for the name Gullege, which still defies explanation, is first recorded in 1351.

By then it was the property of the Alfrey family, who from at least 1287 had lived in the borough of East Grinstead. In the period 1360 to 1478 they five times provided one of the town's Members of Parliament. At the same time they were steadily acquiring lands in the surrounding countryside and eventually a coat of arms also.

The Alfreys moved from Gullege in the mid-17th century and it passed through various hands until becoming by 1876 the home of agricultural labourers. By the mid-20th century, though, it had been rehabilitated as a superior residence and listed grade 2*.

Inevitably such an historic structure became the subject of speculations about tunnels, Henry VIII and Anne Boleyn, for none of which is there a shred of evidence.

The energetic can walk to Imberhorne and Gullege from the town centre by way of Park Road and its continuation Chapmans Lane, returning by the Worth Way, the bridleway created along the former Three Bridges-East Grinstead railway line.

Gullege from the south-east, early in the 20th century, photographed by Arthur Harding and issued by him as a postcard.

FELBRIDGE SCHOOL,
Crawley Down Road, Felbridge (TQ 362396)

Felbridge School, on the A264 in the angle of the Crawley Down and Copthorne roads, incorporates Surrey's oldest school building still in use. It was founded in 1783 by James Evelyn of Felbridge Place to provide free elementary instruction in reading, writing and arithmetic to 12 children living within two and a half miles. Since Felbridge was not then a parish, the catchment area embraced parts of Godstone, East Grinstead, Worth and Horne. One girl aged between six and 13 was to be chosen from each. For boys the age-range was six to 10, three from Godstone, two each from Horne and Worth, and one from East Grinstead. £21 a year was provided for maintenance, insurance and the master's salary. The master, who also had to teach the children how to make their own pens, would have had discretion to take additional paying pupils, for he would not have been able to live on the sum bequeathed.

The original structure, which still sports its original firemark, is typical of local vernacular buildings of the period, with brick walls on the ground floor and a tile-hung timber-framed first storey. It continued to be the head's residence until 1959, originally with kitchen and parlour downstairs alongside the schoolroom and living and sleeping accommodation upstairs. A larger classroom was added in 1810, to a high standard of construction, another extension was created in about 1860, and other additions have regularly been made since. The original premises are now used for administration, with present-day standards of accommodation and facilities in the adjoining classrooms. The school still serves both sides of the county boundary and enjoys a good reputation.

Felbridge School in the early 20th century.

WOODCOCK,
Woodcock Hill, Felbridge (TQ 369405)

Woodcock, originally Woodcock Hill after that part of the A22 on which it stands, about half a mile north of the *Star* junction, was built in about 1902 for Alexander W. Martin, a prosperous London stockbroker. With it went some 25 acres of woodland and fields.

In 1922 Martin's daughter Nancy McIver (pronounced McEever) came to live there with her second husband, known as Suleiman from his service in India. They established a poultry farm but Mrs McIver closed it when he died, before the Second World War, from health problems contracted during the First War.

Having no children, Mrs McIver devoted herself to others, joining the Women's Voluntary Service on its foundation. She represented the village on Godstone Rural District Council from 1949 to 1974 and chaired the meeting in 1953 that led to the formation later that year of Felbridge Parish Council, on which she sat until 1968.

In 1948 she had a house built on the estate for her friends Mr and Mrs Fosse, who had been prisoners of war of the Japanese. When Mr Fosse died in 1969 and Mrs Fosse left, Mrs McIver moved into the ground floor of that house, Little Woodcock, reserving the upper floor for meetings of the Woodcock Housing Association which she then founded. The original house was thereupon converted to six flats, as sheltered housing for five needy elderly people with a Felbridge con-

nection, including a warden's flat, opening in 1970. To thwart any possible nationalisation of such charities, Mrs McIver established a trust to which to leave her assets and bestowed five acres on the Housing Association. In 1981 Mrs McIver moved to East Grinstead and gave Little Woodcock to the association.

Twelve years later she died, two months short of her 100th birthday. McIver Close, built in 1994 off Crawley Down Road, was named to preserve her memory.

Woodcock in June 2005, photographed for this book by S.R. Kerr.

FURTHER READING AND INFORMATION
on those buildings for which anything reliable exists

The publications most often cited are referred to thus:
Bulletin   The *Bulletin* of the East Grinstead Society
Hills   W.H. Hills, *The History of East Grinstead* (1906)

1. A brief guide, illustrated in colour, is on sale. There are fuller accounts in the published histories of East Grinstead and the pre-war church guidebooks.

3. There are articles on Dame Katherine and her husbands and their brass in *Bulletins* 29 and 42 and on these and other almshouses in the town in *Bulletin* 82.

5. The early history of the schools is related in Hills and there is a chronology up to 1975 in *Bulletin* 22.

7. There is a well-illustrated account of the house and its history in volume 6 of the *Sussex County Magazine*, published in 1932. An architectural account appears in *Bulletin* 12 and the medieval and earlier history is reconstructed in *Bulletins* 75, 76 and 79.

8. There is an illustrated account of the house in 1933 in the *Sussex County Magazine*, vol.7. An information leaflet on the estate is sold in the museum.

9. The full story can be read in Dr E.J. Dennison's *A Cottage Hospital Grows Up*. There are several books about Sir Archibald McIndoe (as he became) and the Guinea Pig Club formed by his wartime service patients.

12. Several items relating to the Palmers and Dixons are displayed in the Town Museum.

13. There is a full illustrated account in *Bulletin* 30.

14. There is more detail on the cycle businesses in *Bulletins* 65, 68 and 69.

16. There are several books about Neale, who has been described as 'perhaps the most brilliant and versatile priest of the Church of England in the nineteenth century', of which the most recent is *The Life and Work of John Mason Neale* by Michael Chandler (Gracewing, 1995). A history of the College was produced by Neale in 1853, and in 1913 there appeared *Sackville College by the twenty-second Warden* (Frank Hill, an American). A short illustrated guide is on sale in the College.

18. There is a full illustrated account of both the house and the gate-lodges by the architectural historian Doreen Yarwood in *Bulletin* 43. The Felbridge & District History Group has published a pamphlet on Lutyens's work in that village. More generally Lutyens has been the subject of many books and articles in architectural periodicals.

20. There is an article on the house and the policemen stationed there in *Bulletin* 80.

23. The hunting scene is illustrated and discussed in *Bulletins* 46 and 47, together with other fragments of wall-painting in our High Street.

24. There are articles on Geoffrey Webb in *Bulletin* 19 and his assistant Thomas Vivian Smith in *Bulletin* 53.

25. R.T. Mason's account appears in *Sussex Archaeological Collections*, volume 80. Recent re-investigation and the documentary history are fully written up in *Bulletin* 81.

26. There are accounts of Dorset House including its predecessor and its restoration, in *Bulletins* 45 and 46.

30. There is a full account of the building's structural and documentary history in *Bulletin* 80.

31. There is an account of the demolished building, including a drawing of its probable original appearance, in *Bulletin* 1.

36. There is a full account of the building's structural and documentary history in *Bulletin* 79 and an article discussing the rash of re-building in the 1450s in *Bulletin* 74.

38. A full account of the structural and documentary history of the building will be found in *Bulletin* 77.

39. A full account of the structural and documentary history of the building will be found in *Bulletin* 82.

40. A full account of the structural and documentary history of the building will be found in *Bulletin* 83, Mrs Dempster's memories of her childhood there in the booklet of reminiscences published by the East Grinstead Society in 1973, and recollections of Dr Walker by one of his former scouts in the Museum Society's *Newsletter* 45.

42. There is a booklet about the chapel, *This and That, 1811-1961*, and it is occasionally opened for public viewing.

44. There is an illustrated account of the cemetery and the chapels in *Bulletin* 49.

45. The viaduct, and the whole story of the line up to 1958, is exhaustively treated in K. Marx's *An Illustrated History of the Lewes and East Grinstead Railway*.

48. Detailed articles on the structural and documentary history of the building will be found in *Bulletins* 75, 76 and 77, the excavations at its

rear in *Bulletin* 80, and the history of the hardware business that became a sweet-shop in *Bulletin* 85.

49. There is an article on the earlier history of the site, known as Bedlams Bank, in *Bulletin* 32 and a full historical account of the cinema in Tony Hounsome's *Threepennyworth of Dark*. M.J. Leppard's *A History of East Grinstead* tells the story of the bombing.

51. Hills gives an account of Thomas Cramp and prints extracts from his diary.

53. There is an article on the building in *Bulletin* 5. A centenary history was published in 1971. (Anyone curious about the 'moat' names is referred to *Bulletins* 50 and 77.)

55. There are articles on the 19th-century development of Lingfield Road in *Bulletin* 67 and on Wellington Town in *Bulletin* 77.

58. A detailed illustrated account of the church was published in the *Sussex County Magazine* volume 3 in 1929.

60. There is a full illustrated account of the structural and documentary history of the building in *Bulletin* 41.

62. There are articles on the bridge and the river in *East Grinstead Museum Compass* no.9.

64. There is an article on Lingfield Lodge in *Bulletin* 85.

66. Wood's article about the Pennifolds and the building can be read in *Bulletin* 19.

67. Readers too young or too new to the area to have seen our rail network in its heyday will find plenty of books of photographs. The most detailed accounts, including plans and track layouts, are David Gould's *Three Bridges to Tunbridge Wells* and *The Croydon, Oxted and East Grinstead Railway* and Klaus Marx's *Illustrated History of the Lewes and East Grinstead Railway*.

68. There is an illustrated account of the *Railway Hotel* and its successor in *Bulletin* 28.

73. An article on the development of Moat Road in the 19th century in *Bulletin* 77 gives detailed accounts of all its houses and their occupiers, including Oak Croft and today's Springvale.

74. There is an anonymous booklet on the community's work in East Grinstead, *Doing the Impossible*, and a history of the order's world-wide work, *The Planting of the Lord*, by Sister Catherine Louise of the autonomous American Society. *Convent Memories* is an illustrated account by Sylvia Spencer, a niece of the artist Stanley Spencer, of her childhood in the sisters' orphanage at the old convent.

75. The Gatehouse and Dovecotes are the subject of an illustrated article in *Bulletin* 26.

77. An account of the structural history, including plans, is in *Bulletin* 5.

78. There is much in print on Standen, including a substantial detailed guidebook and history with many illustrations published by the National Trust.

81. There is a detailed history of the school in the periodical *Forest Row, Historical Aspects and Recollections*, volume 1, parts 2 and 3.

82. There are detailed accounts of the history of Kidbrooke by E.C. Byford, a long-serving member of the Michael Hall staff, in the periodical he founded and edited, *Forest Row, Historical Aspects and Recollections*, volume 1, parts 3 and 4.

83. There are detailed accounts of the church in R.P. Odell's booklet *The Parish of Forest Row, 1836-1962* and E.C. Byford's articles in *Forest Row, Historical Aspects and Recollections*, volume 3, parts 3 and 4.

84. There is a full, illustrated account of the *Swan* in *Forest Row, Historical Aspects and Recollections*, volume 3, part 1.

88. There are fuller accounts of the *Three Crowns* in Bulletin 35 and in *Ashurst Wood, 1086-1986*.

89. There are accounts of various aspects of Little Shovelstrode Hall's history in *Bulletins* 28, 29, 58 and 65.

90. A booklet on the house by Mr Pinnegar is on sale, supplementing his guided tours. An illustrated account by the architectural historian Doreen Yarwood will be found in *Bulletin* 48.

91. Ashdown House can be read about in the illustrated *History of Ashdown House* by Christopher Richmond, which deals fully with the building, the estate and the school. There is an architectural account by Doreen Yarwood in *Bulletin* 48, including drawings of Latrobe's Greek models.

94. Virtually all that can be known about Kingscote station will be found in Klaus Marx's detailed and authoritative *Illustrated History of the Lewes and East Grinstead Railway*.

95. There are illustrated accounts of Tickeridge by R.T. Mason in *Sussex Archaeological Collections* volumes 82 and 95.

96. A structural account and history of Gravetye Manor, by Mrs Kay Coutin and the late Peter Gray, has been published by the Wealden Buildings Study Group.

97. A full history of Imberhorne Farm has been produced by the Felbridge and District History Group.

98. A fully referenced account of all that is known for certain of the history of Gullege and of the Alfreys connected with it will be found in *Bulletin* 76.

99. To mark the bicentenary of Felbridge School a good, well-illustrated, history was written by Mr Gordon Wilkinson, including reminiscences from 1894 onwards. The book also contains some general historical material to make it suitable for classroom use as well as of interest to adults.

INDEX OF BUILDINGS AND PLACE-NAMES
including entries in 'Further Reading and Information'

The numbers that follow are not of pages but of the hundred featured buildings, whose main entries are indicated by **bold** type under both current and earlier or alternative names. Non-local place-names are indexed selectively, depending on their relevance to the history and architecture of the local buildings included. AW = Ashurst Wood, Fb = Felbridge, FR = Forest Row. All other local addresses (except Gravetye) are East Grinstead.

INDEX OF PERSONAL NAMES
including entries in 'Further Reading and Information'

The numbers that follow are not of pages but of the hundred featured buildings. In the text names are usually given as used at the time or found in the sources. In the index they are amplified where possible, except for persons alive at the time of writing. It has not always been possible to distinguish different persons of the same name. Persons named in the captions to illustrations are indexed, including photographers. Architects are indicated by **bold** print, builders and masons by *italics*. Other artists or craftsmen who contributed to the structures listed are indicated in words. An asterisk (*) indicates a portrait.